TAMING THE DRAGON IN YOUR CHILD

Other books coauthored by Sydney Craft Rozen

Dinosaur Brains: Dealing with All Those Impossible People at Work
(with Albert J. Bernstein, Ph.D.)

*Neanderthals at Work: How People and Politics Can Drive You Crazy . . .
And What You Can Do About Them* (with Albert J. Bernstein, Ph.D.)

TAMING THE DRAGON IN YOUR CHILD

SOLUTIONS FOR BREAKING THE CYCLE OF FAMILY ANGER

Meg Eastman, Ph.D.
with
Sydney Craft Rozen

John Wiley & Sons, Inc.

New York • Chichester • Brisbane • Toronto • Singapore

Copyright © 1994 by Anne Margaret Eastman and Sydney Craft Rozen.
Published by John Wiley & Sons, Inc.

First Wiley mass market edition published 1997

Library of Congress Cataloging-in-Publication Data:

Eastman, Meg.
    Taming the dragon in you child : solutions for breaking the cycle of family anger / Meg Eastman, Sydney Craft Rozen.
        p. cm.
        Includes index.
    ISBN 0-471-59405-9 (acid-free paper)
            0-471-17692-3 (mass market)
    1. Anger in children. 2. Temper tantrums in children. 3. Child Rearing. I.Rozen, Sydney Craft.   II. Title.
    BF723.A4E38   1994
    649'.64—dc20   93-13316

Printed in the United States of America

10 9 8 7 6 5 4 3 2 1

CONTENTS

PREFACE

Parents ask, *What do we do about temper tantrums? How do we handle children who are out of control? How do we teach children to express anger without hurting other people?* These are important questions. Adults need specific, practical answers about how to stop angry tirades and teach children to express anger responsibly.

Millions of parents of normal children will welcome a book filled with ideas, strategies, and examples of how to handle anger in children of all ages. This book is intended for them. It will also be a valuable resource for the more than one million parents who seek professional guidance each year for their children.

I have spent ten years conceiving and refining my ideas for this book. I wanted to share advice about how to stop, and learn from, the angry explosions that drive parents crazy. The advice I offer is based on the struggles and successes of thousands of parents who have worked with me to Tame the Dragon.

Often when I am introduced as a child psychologist, other parents joke, "Oh, then your kids must be perfect." I laugh, because none of us is perfect, but we all want to be perfect parents. From experience, I realize that knowing what to do is very different from actually succeeding in the heat of anger. When we are angry and out of control, we all do and say things we later regret. We forget our new skills and resort to habits that have been our family's patterns of anger for generations.

Information in Part I, "Meeting the Dragon," will help you understand the roots of your own anger, the "Dragons" that families pass from one generation to the next. In addition you will learn to assess your parenting and problem-solving style, as well as learn new ways to express anger and resolve conflicts. Families facing special challenges, such as divorce, school problems, abuse, death, or other highly stressful circumstances, will find needed advice, as well as guidelines for deciding whether professional intervention is appropriate. It should be noted that Chapter 5, "Two-Parent Families: Problem-Solving Styles," includes information that is relevant for the many configurations of today's two-parent families. Chapter 6 reflects the struggles and successes of single-parent families.

Part II, "As the Dragon Grows," supplies important information about children's development and how the Dragon of Anger appears in each stage. In Part III, "Old and New Dragon Patterns," you will first assess your old, negative dragonlike anger reactions; then you will learn how to create new patterns that provide realistic, workable ways to deal with the inevitable tantrums, blowups, and arguments that are normal parts of family life.

Part IV provides more specific strategies to communicate, discipline, and resolve conflicts for toddlers to teens. Special chapters on helping your child learn to handle conflicts at school and with siblings also appear.

Part V contains three chapters on children who provide special challenges to parents. Finally, Part VI recaps what you have learned about Taming the Dragon and encourages celebrating your steps toward peace. The end of the book contains appendixes with important resource information for parents who want to learn more or need additional help.

The most important reason to read this book is that the strategies and suggestions here will give your family the strength and confidence to handle anger in a new spirit of cooperation and hope. The advice for change is based on research findings in child development and family psychology, as well on the personal struggles we all face as parents. Our children grow and change. So do we as parents. Families, and the people within them, *can* Tame the Dragon. This book will show you how.

Meg Eastman, Ph.D.

ACKNOWLEDGMENTS

Meg Eastman sends many thanks to all those near and dear. Your gifts have helped me master my own Dragons of Anger and given me the opportunity to write about what works. You have led me to the following truths about anger and about life.

My grandparents taught me that nothing is more important than nurturing life and love. Patience and the joys of giving, and forgiving, will help us all weather the storms of anger.

My parents gave me a strong security base, so that I developed self-reliance and sensitivity to the rights of others. These tools have spurred me to master the art of compromise and negotiation. Blessed with the confidence that I could do anything, I wanted to teach others the tools of peacemaking.

My colleagues at the Children's Program in Portland, at Oregon Health Sciences University, West Virginia University, and Virginia Tech gave me the nourishment and support to effectively help families who are mired in conflict. The tools and strategies developed in this book come through the stimulating opportunity of working with such wonderful folks.

My husband lovingly reminds me that, with a deep commitment and a sense of shared purpose, even the most fiery conflict or the iciest cold war can pass. Joy and harmony can reign.

My daughter teaches me daily that conflicts are inevitable as we struggle to grow and love. What could be better than hysterical, and contagious, giggles after one of my particularly ridiculous tizzy fits?

"My" families, who have trusted themselves to the daring process of therapy, have kept me eternally optimistic. Conflicts bring a wonderful opportunity to change, to those brave enough to try.

My writing partner, Sydney, has transformed this book: Her warmth and positive energy echo within. What better compliment to the book than to hear Sydney, the loving mother of two very normal children, say, "Boy, has this book made me a better parent!"

PART I
MEETING THE DRAGON

1

The Dragon's Many Faces

Remember the splendid purple and green dragon in your child's favorite scary storybook? On one page, the raging beast breathed fire upon the cowering knights who dared to cross his path. On the next page, the fearsome creature tramped, in cold silence, back to his lair. Toward the end of the story, the sleeping dragon lay, curled into a corner of his cave, claws sheathed, scaly wings furled, enchanting and harmless—until he awakened again.

Anger Lurks in Every Family

Like the many-mooded dragon in children's literature, the Dragon of Anger has many faces within a family.

When children feel angry, hurt, disappointed, or frustrated, they want the world to know. How they express their anger depends on their age and temperament, and on the anger patterns they have learned from their parents.

Likewise, all parents get angry, even those who have promised themselves that they would never, ever use their words or their bodies as weapons against their children. Yet, when faced with a child's uncontrolled rage, it is natural to want to strike back. You may be ashamed to admit that sometimes you want to slay the Dragon (or at least to stifle your child). You may want to banish the Dragon forever (or at least punish your child or confine her to a time-out chair). If nothing seems to work, you feel powerless—and more angry.

Even when you know what you *should* do to calm your angry child, it's often difficult to find the patience to work things out. Heaven knows, there are no perfect parents. Anyone who has ever nurtured a child knows that we all do and say things that we are ashamed of later. All of us have stooped to screaming, foot-stomping, and threats. We may find ourselves resorting to the same angry tirades that we find so inappropriate in our children. We all feel like strangling the kids at times, or walking away and letting somebody else deal with them. Many of us end up following—and thereby teaching our children—the same patterns *we* learned.

Family Anger Patterns

Anger patterns—each family's personal Dragons—are familiar because you probably learned them from your own parents. You saw these patterns repeated at home so many times that you automatically fell into the same behavior as you grew up. Now you may be worrying that you have become a "dysfunctional" family, despite your best intentions. Many parents find themselves handing down these Dragons to their own children and wondering, *WHY is everybody so mad all the time?*

Children, howver, operate on a different level from adults. They don't tend to stew about *why* they are mad. They aren't looking for deep explanations. They just know that they're angry—or that Mom or Dad is fuming. Children may sense the connections between their anger, or yours, and its consequences, but they are helpless to start new patterns. That will be *your* job as a parent: to learn and teach new, healthy ways to handle anger. By changing your family's anger patterns, you will be resolving your child's anger problem—and your own.

You can find an important message in your child's fairy tales about angry dragons. *Conflict and anger are a normal part of family life.* When the fire-breathing rage begins at your house, you can cower in fear, you can be perpetually at war, or you can master the Dragon of Anger. When you anticipate conflicts and see that a tantrum is building, you can use the suggestions in this book to deal with the problem more calmly and to reach a resolution. Taming the Dragon begins with a commitment to changing your old patterns and creating a happy ending to your own family story.

2

Anger

UNDERSTANDING ITS ROOTS

As difficult as it can be to live with anger, it is impossible to live without it. Anger can be a powerful motivator for change, in yourself and in your child. The goal of this book is not to stop your family's angry emotions, but to help your family recognize, understand, and control anger, and to express it constructively. Easier said than done? Of course. Impossible? No—you *can* do it! Essential for your children? Yes, if you want to help create caring adults who are capable of satisfying relationships.

Anger-Related Problems

You can begin to understand the powerful emotion of anger and its effect on your own family by reading the following summaries, which discuss the causes and roots of several anger-related problems.

Gender Differences in Anger

Even in this age of concern about equality, we continue to have different expectations for girls than for boys. Parents and teachers tend to respond differently when a boy or a girl gets angry. We are more likely to expect and excuse an aggressive outburst in a boy and a tantrum of frustrated crying in a girl. The reality is that children of both sexes need to learn to handle their anger without violence or manipulation. Aggression is just one way to express anger or to get what you want. Certainly we can teach our children more peaceful and cooperative responses.

Although studies confirm that young boys are more likely to be active and rowdy, boys are just as able as girls to learn safe, effective ways to cope with frustration and relieve tension. As children grow, actions and words become crucial tools for calming rages and resolving conflicts. However, the actions and words that our culture teaches them to use when they are angry may be quite different for girls. For example, boys often earn peer recognition for their physical feats—athletic skills and the ability to punch out an "enemy." (We would have to be blind in our culture to be unaware of the rampant examples and reinforcement of violence in males in the media.) Girls, however, often earn status for their appearance or for taking leading roles in promoting group harmony.

There are significant differences in the ways adults respond to anger in girls and anger in boys. We are much more likely to expect and excuse an aggressive outburst in a boy, inadvertently reinforcing its use. We are more likely to respond to a girl's frustrated crying with support, but to tell a boy not to cry. Most parents urge their daughters to talk out problems and to turn the other cheek of kindness. But would the same parents also encourage their sons to handle frustrations and conflicts peacefully, or would they urge their boys to fight for their rights?

These sex-role stereotypes may begin in the preschool years, but they seem to become nearly carved in stone during elementary school. Identification with same-sex friends is universal. Parents may buy dolls for boys and trucks for girls, but by age eight, few children willingly cross the traditional gender lines. Status, belonging, and esteem depend on fitting into the peer group.

Nevertheless, parents *can* teach children of both genders to control their bodies and use words to solve problems. They can show boys and girls how to share, and how to use words to handle frustrations and to solve problems.

Chapter 27 provides additional information for parents who have an aggressive child.

Aggression

Children want to be in control. As they learn to be in charge of themselves, they can go overboard trying to control everyone else. Aggression is a learned reaction, one of the most common manifestations of the Dragon. We learn aggressive behavior and pass it on to the next generation because attack is often "effective." Does might really make right? Do the strongest and loudest win?

> *"It's MINE!"* is three-year-old Joey's battle cry. If another child tries to share the same toy, Joey will stake his territory by pushing or hitting. What can his parents and preschool teacher do to help him control his aggressiveness before another child gets hurt? Is this just a passing stage or a sign that something is wrong?

Tantrums

Children whose parents tolerate and reinforce (even indirectly) their tantrums will be at risk for emotional problems as an adult. When children learn that whining, crying, and sulking are powerful ways to get others to do what they want *now*, they become self-centered and demanding adults.

> *Bedtimes have become a real battle ground for seven-year-old Heather and her parents. As soon as her mom or dad calls out, "Time for bed, honey," Heather launches into an all-out tantrum, whining and crying that she doesn't want to go to bed and she won't go to bed. Her parents, who feel guilty for the long hours they spend at their jobs, worry that Heather's tantrums are really her way of saying, "You're not spending enough time with me."*
>
> *They draw out the bedtime ritual, soothing, reading to and sitting with Heather as they wait for her calm down. Yet no matter how long they stay, their little girl still cannot seem to fall asleep alone—and the next night, the bedtime tantrum begins again. Everyone is so irritable from lack of sleep that they feel like raging dragons. What's going on?*

You can learn to take the power out of tantrums so that your child will have no motivation to use them. You can stop letting your child push your buttons, and you don't have to feel paralyzed by guilt. Parents can teach their young children effective coping skills and help them soothe and control themselves, even when they are physically out of control. Chapters 9, 16, and 17 will provide more specific tips on dealing with tantrums and teaching self-calming strategies.

Violence

Common sense (and history) tells us that the most frequent targets of our anger are those we hate. Wars, violent revenge, aggression, and destruction—this drama of hatred is all too characteristic of the human society. Individuals, however, are much more likely to respond with anger and aggression toward those they love. Our society's rates of murder, child abuse, and domestic violence indicate the grave risk of aggression that can fester and explode within a family.

Children who are exposed to violent adults are at great risk to become violent adults themselves. Because they are powerless to stop the cycle of aggressive anger, children begin to identify with the aggressor. No one is there to teach them how to resolve conflict with cooperation. Anger becomes their reason for revenge, retaliation, and hurtful attacks. The cycle of pain grows and continues to the next generation. The reality of anger is that we most often hurt the ones we love.

Almost every parent has used a quick swat, particularly with a toddler in danger of hurting herself or himself. But although a swat may be immediately effective, it is *not* appropriate in the long run. Excessive and inappropriate expressions of anger create their own problems. Bullying, tantrums, insults, and threats always move the Dragon of Anger toward an explosion. You, as a caring parent, should not encourage, use, or tolerate verbal or physical aggression as a response to anger.

> *Justin and Jason were born only fifteen months apart. When they were toddlers, their wrestling and tickling matches seemed like good ways to burn off extra energy and promote "male bonding." If their rough-housing got out of hand, a quick swat on their bottoms quickly separated them. When the boys reached school age, their conflicts grew more intense and violent. If their parents tried to stop the fracas, the boys started a heated argument over "who started it," until their exasperated mom or dad would slap both of them and send them to their rooms.*
>
> *As preteens, Justin and Jason couldn't even ride in the car to the grocery store without shouting and hitting. Teachers and other parents often called to report a fight. The two brothers also were reported to be hanging out with possible gang members. What could their parents do to stop their sons' pattern of increasing violence? Was it dangerous, or would they grow out of it? Was there hope, or had their problem gone too far?*

Children must learn that violence is *never* an acceptable way to deal with anger in the family. Parents can discipline effectively and set limits so that violence does not occur. The tools in this book will help you and your child solve conflicts without violence. Your child can then use these tools to handle conflicts with peers. He can be cool and earn status and control by being calm. The chapters in Part 4 provide many strategies for parents to help them teach their children conflict-resolution skills.

Moodiness and Blowups

At times, anger is justified. However, children often show anger when they are really feeling hurt, sad, left out, disappointed, inadequate, jealous, or overwhelmed.

Anger can mask vulnerability and help a child feel tough and strong. But the anger can confuse and push away parents who want to help. Parents become targets of the rage and feel wounded, vulnerable, and confused, just like their child. Parents worry, *Is there something seriously troubling my child? But how can I find out, when every attempt I make to understand just leads to more moodiness, sulks, and explosions? Will these power struggles ever end?* Understanding children's developmental stages (see Chapter 3 and Part II: Chapters 8 to 12) will give parents insights into when children are more apt to go through a moody or volatile phase.

> *Nate had always been strong-willed, but now, at twelve, his anger and moodiness were becoming unbearable. He had to be right and blamed everyone for everything. His parents realized that Nate faced new pressures and strains as he entered junior high, but they still found it so difficult to weather his storms. He always seemed to be angry. The simplest request seemed to trigger a blowup and a slammed-door retreat to his room.*
>
> *Nate was so moody and unpredictable that his parents worried he might be on drugs. Bewildered and overwhelmed, his parents tried asking sympathetic questions, ignoring his outbursts, lecturing, and, finally, grounding him. Nothing worked. Was there a way to reach Nate, or would the family have to live through the next six years in a war zone?*

How do you help a child who rejects your attempts? The teen who doesn't care; who doesn't want to listen; who always insists he is right? Our own feelings are no more real or more valid than those of the child or adult with whom we are angry. Teaching respect for the rights of others and sensitivity to others' feelings is a very important goal you can reach by Taming the Dragon of Anger. Children can learn to handle pressures and gain positive self-esteem by being in control of their feelings.

Teen Pressures

The teen years can be shattering times. Even the most easygoing teens feel overwhelmed at times. Stress can build. The balancing act of juggling feelings, responsibilities, and the needs of others can sometimes seem like just too much.

> *Sixteen-year-old Maria had seemed like such a saint—sweet-tempered and kind. But dating had changed her. Boys called constantly, pressuring her to go out. Her parents had given her information about sexuality, abstinence, and birth control, but now, when faced with real possibilities, they worried about the choices Maria would make. Her parents' concerns just seemed like one more pressure to Maria, who grew increasingly antagonistic and withdrawn.*
>
> *Although she had always been close to her family, Maria never had time any more for anything but school, her job, and the boys. Her parents wanted to trust that she could handle it all, but they became more and more worried. Spats with boyfriends were so intensely*

fiery that Maria seemed out of control. She had been cheerful and responsible at work, but now her boss was reprimanding her for "attitude problems." Even worse, Maria tried to hide her problems from her parents. When they confronted her, she slammed the shower door so hard that the glass shattered.

Could Maria really be expected to make mature decisions about her problems, or did her parents need to take charge?

Nearly all parents are terrified that their teens may be deeply hurt by mistakes made while exercising newfound freedom. It is hard to know when to take charge and when to let go. Control battles can lead to blowups and alienation.

You can help your angry teenager gain independence and success. Stress management, negotiation, and problem-solving skills are the keys to Taming the Dragon at this stage. Maturing teens are ready to become moral, caring, and responsible if parents know how to lead the way.

Anger as a Motivator

You may be reading this book because your child's intense or inappropriate anger is troubling you. There is a bright side to the problem. Your child has motivated you! Change *is* possible. For example, anger can move you to recognize needs and respond. Anger can be an effective release of tension. Anger can cue you to correct wrongs. Anger, used effectively, can get results. Thus, anger can force you to grow, adapt, and change.

By reading this book, you will learn to recognize and deal with the pressures and frustrations that create anger build-ups in yourself and your child. You will be able to help your child express anger appropriately, and break the cycle of arguing that leads to bitterness and resentment. As you learn ways to tame the Dragon of Anger in your family, you will be able to give up unrealistic expectations and destructive patterns that left you feeling frustrated, paralyzed, or hopeless.

Although this book will help you get started and will keep you moving forward by setting and reaching realistic, step-by-step goals, it asks you to change *your* perspective *before your child can change*. You may be able to reason your way through a flare-up, but logic is beyond a child who's in a fit of rage. Taking a "child's-eye view" of anger can give you new answers.

When children know that grownups hear—and really understand—what they say, they become more willing to listen. As your own understanding and confidence grow, you will be able to give your child a sense of security and safety. Then conflicts will stop being angry battles and become opportunities for change.

You *can* Tame the Dragon in your family. But please don't expect immediate results. Be realistic about the slow process of change. Give the ideas you read about time to percolate. Modify them to suit your family's individual style and situation. As you learn what's normal and what's not, you will become confident and able to take charge effectively when the Dragon comes out of its cave.

By reading this book, you will learn to recognize and deal with the pressures and frustrations that create anger build-ups in yourself and your child. You will be able to help your child express anger without being mean, and break the cycle of arguing that leads to bitterness and resentment. As you learn ways to tame the Dragon of Anger in your family, you will be able to give up unrealistic expectations and destructive patterns that left you feeling frustrated, paralyzed or hopeless.

3

What Is "Normal" Anger?

Anger has so many triggers and causes that it can be difficult to understand it, much less figure out what to do about it. Parents can become paralyzed by guilt and indecision. You can be so blinded by your own anger that you just want to attack. You may worry so much about the "real" cause of your child's anger that you can fail to take appropriate action. Unless you start the process of change, the Dragon of Anger will grow stronger and more destructive.

Your child, like all kids, has probably reached a stage that includes significant problems with anger and temper outbursts. (Some kids seem to spend their entire childhoods in a tantrum.) Intellectually, you know that anger is a normal way for children (and adults) to express rage, hurt, fear, confusion, and frustration. But when your child's angry feelings come out in tirades or seem to last forever, you need help.

Maybe your family is going through a period of extreme stress, and it doesn't take much to send tempers flaring.

Maybe your child is in the middle of a normal, but still frustrating, anger-laced stage that none of your parenting books seems to explain.

Or maybe your child has begun to display flashes of more intense rage that leave you worried and baffled, asking yourself, *Why did this happen? Am I a bad parent? Why is my child acting like this? What can I do to help? Is my child justifiably angry, or do I have a perpetually Angry Child?*

Most of all, you are probably wondering, *Is all this anger normal? Are we just going through a stage, or does my child have a serious problem with anger? And how can I tell the difference?*

Anger becomes a problem in a family when:

- it is too frequent.
- it is too intense.
- it lasts too long.
- it leads to aggression.
- it masks other feelings.
- it disturbs family and work relationships.
- it begins a destructive cycle that we do not control.
- it hurts people.

Anger Triggers

Some kids are constantly angry. Every little thing triggers a battle or an explosion. What makes children angry, and when does their anger become a problem? As a parent, if you can answer this question, you are well on your way to finding solutions that work.

By looking at the following *triggers* of anger and considering how your child responds, you can decide whether your child has a problem with anger.

Pressures

The stress of daily life can overwhelm even small children. Hurry, hurry! Rush, rush! Teenagers can have so many competing demands that they have a hard time knowing how to juggle them all. *It is normal to blow off steam when we have had a hard day.* Kids are legitimately angry when the pressures have gotten to be too much, and they feel out of control.

Anger becomes a problem when kids cannot cope with the pressures. If a child is constantly overloaded, she may seem perpetually resentful, moody, and explosive. Rage becomes her pressure release. Unfortunately, these destructive rages backfire because they add more stress. The child spends so much energy on the battles that she has nothing left for trying to handle the pressures or solving the problem.

As the conflict heats up, you, the parent, can feel so overwhelmed with battling her rage that you have no time or energy to find out what is causing her anger or to help prevent it from happening.

Conflicts

All families have conflicts. Brothers and sisters compete for attention and needs. Parents make demands that the children cannot (or simply aren't in the mood to) fulfill. Frustrations and disagreements create tensions that lead to anger. *It is normal to feel angry during a conflict.* The anger can lead to solutions, if parents know how to lead their children to compromises and constructive actions.

Anger becomes a problem if kids cannot resolve conflicts peacefully. Some kids always have a chip on their shoulder. They cannot compromise, or even agree to disagree and call a truce. They use words as weapons, rather than as tools of peace. If they cannot get their way with words, they will use physical force. Solutions seem unreachable when they are focused on revenge. These angry children seem more interested in winning the war at all costs than in creating peace.

Developmental Stages

Children go through predictable stages as they develop. As you will read in Chapters 8, 9, 10 and 11, anger is inevitable as children struggle to master their changing bodies and feelings. *Anger is normal as children enter new stages and learn new things.* You, as a parent, have to keep readjusting the line between what *you* need to do and what your child is now ready to do for herself. Battles over control help families decide who is in charge of what now.

As children develop, however, they must learn self-discipline. They need to understand that it is OK to feel angry but that growing up means that they must master their out-of-control anger and learn to make peace with themselves and others.

Anger becomes a problem when children do not develop the skills to be masters of their own anger. Dangerously angry children can become stuck in the toddlers' mentality: *Might makes right. Me first!* Aggression and power take top priority. Explosive children have not learned to master their own bodies so that they can *calm* themselves in a fit of rage. Aggressive children have not yet learned that *words can solve problems* and that *everyone can win.*

Low Self-Esteem

Satisfaction with who we are and how we are loved is a vital part of family life. *It is normal for all of us to feel left out, inadequate, jealous, or abandoned at times.* When we feel wounded, we can all be tempted to lash out with vicious criticisms or seething curses. Blaming and shaming lead to more wounds. Sharing feelings and being understood can build closeness and satisfaction that we are loved.

It is normal for very young children to express sadness and loss through angry tantrums. Children often express sadness as anger. As they grow, however, it is essential that they learn to handle hurt and pain constructively.

Anger can become a serious problem for the wounded child. Trauma, divorce, death, and abuse can cause deep hurt. Pain can seem so overwhelming that nothing seems to matter. Children can mistakenly believe that no one can help. They may try to show others how much they are hurting by trying to hurt back. Especially sad is that their rage often pushes away those who love them and want to help. It can be very painful to reach out to try to help your child and to have him attack again with another fit of rage.

Is Your Child an Angry Child?

The following checklist will help you determine whether your child has become an Angry Child. The more statements that describe your child, the more likely it is that he or she has a problem with anger.

Your child:

____ blows when pressure builds.

____ can't handle change and stress.

____ shows rage when troubled by loss, pain, hurt, frustration, or disappointment.

____ turns anger into shouting, tantrums, or aggression.

____ can't calm down when he or she is angered.

____ fights with others frequently.

____ uses words as weapons.

____ blames others.

____ thrives on revenge.

____ will not take responsibility.

____ lacks self-control.

____ has a low self-confidence.

____ doesn't seem to care about others' feelings and rights.

____ won't compromise.

____ can't negotiate.

Are You an Angry Parent?

Don't despair! We all have days when we believe we could have checked every item on the previous list (and every item on the list that follows). The more you can recognize and understand about your child's and your own anger patterns, the better able you will be to change yourself and you child.

The following checklist will help you decide whether you have an anger problem.

As a parent, you:

____ feel the family conflict and turmoil will never end.

____ overreact to minor squabbles and tensions.

____ feel overwhelmed by too many demands and pressures.

____ have no time or way to relax.

____ don't know how much anger is normal because you might have grown up in a dysfunctional family.

____ are confused about what to expect as your child reaches different ages and stages.

____ become triggered to rage by your child's anger.

____ become panicked and paralyzed by your child's anger.

____ argue with your spouse, or your own parents, about your child.

____ can't admit you have made mistake.

____ are afraid to apologize.

____ find it impossible to compromise.

____ have become a referee or a police officer to your children.

____ punish, rather than encourage discussion and understanding.

____ place respect for your own authority above mutual respect.

____ never see problems get solved.

____ can't create a climate of peace in your family.

How you respond to anger is crucial to Taming the Dragon. In Chapters 4 to 7, you will learn more about understanding and changing your own angry feelings. Your goal will be to teach your child to respond to anger with self-control.

You *can* become a peacemaker. You can teach your child to master the raging Dragon and become a calm, effective communicator and problem solver.

4

Parenting Styles and Anger

To a child, a parent's hot temper is the biggest Dragon of them all.

When you are the target of your child's anger, it's natural to want to lash out and retaliate. Remember, though, before you strike back, that your verbal attacks carry a power far more destructive than any childish rage.

No matter how irresponsible and out-of-control you may feel at times, you, the parent, are ultimately responsible for how you and your child express anger at home, at school, and in your community. Certainly this is a huge responsibility, but you won't be alone as you tackle it. You can draw on your sense of humor, your deep well of love for your child, and a dragon's lair full of ideas, information, and advice from this book. You will be able to control anger, first in yourself, then in your child.

Maybe you're worrying that you are the cause of your child's problems, and that your family's anger is too complex and too long-standing to be resolved. Instead of letting your guilt paralyze you, use it as a motivator. By changing your expectations and reducing the stresses on yourself and your child, you can begin the process of change. Love, humor, and understanding can Tame the Dragon. If you keep trying, you *will* create positive changes for your child and yourself.

Four Typical Parenting Styles

As you read the following descriptions and examples, you'll probably recognize yourself several times. Remember, the key to a healthy self-examination is maintaining your sense of humor, your sense of reality, and as much objectivity as you can bring to the problem of coping with conflict and anger. You are not to blame for old patterns, but you are responsible for finding solutions.

The Appeaser: Let the Dragon Have Its Way

The Appeaser style of parenting is widely thought to be a vestige of the "let it all hang out" philosophy of the 1960s, but it has far deeper roots in our culture. The common theme of permissive parents of all eras is that children are unique and precious beings whose goodness will in time blossom and emerge.

"Appeaser" Parents:

- place high value on freedom of expression, both verbal and artistic.
- believe that children will naturally show altruistic and caring tendencies.
- think anger and other "negative" emotions should be accepted as expressions of the child's creativity. If the child has a tantrum or otherwise expresses anger inappropriately, Appeasers think a rational discussion will be enough to motivate the child to become more caring and responsible.
- may fail to set appropriate boundaries and limits for fear of stifling the child.

The Appeaser style may work well with a child who is sensitive to and aware of the rights of others, but it is inappropriate for a highly physical child who is easily angered and difficult to console. Expecting this child to respond to reason and persuasion is inappropriate and unfair. In the heat of explosive anger, a "physical" child needs limits and boundaries. Without this safety net, the child will become increasingly out of control and push even the most passive parent to take action.

> Seven-year-old Ryan burst in to the living room, where his parents were hosting a cocktail party. He made a beeline for the hors d'oeuvres, stuffed several into his mouth, then dashed to the piano and announced (through a flying spray of cheese-straw crumbs), "I will now entertain you!"
>
> As Ryan loudly plunked a discordant jangle of notes, several annoyed guests turned expectantly toward his parents, waiting for them to scoop up their ill-behaved child and put him to bed. Instead, Ryan's mother hesitantly placed her hand on his shoulder and said, "Ryan, honey, maybe it's time to end your recital now and say good night to our nice friends. . . ."
>
> Ryan angrily shook off his mother's hand and bellowed, "NO! I want to play the piano!" Ryan's parents exchanged fond, helpless

smiles, shrugged and let the concert continue. "You know," Ryan's mother whispered to a nearby guest, "Ryan is a gifted child."

King of the Mountain: Might Equals Right

At the other end of the style spectrum from the Appeasers are the parents who serve as rulers or dictators of the household. They believe that their authority *must* be unconditionally respected.

"King of the Mountain" Parents:

- expect their children to obey all adult-imposed rules and to meet adult expectations.
- set very firm boundaries. When a rule is violated, punishment is swift and sure.
- allow no room in the rules for flexibility, negotiation, or response from the child. Rigid in their need for control, these parents often cannot tolerate the growing child's attempts to establish control.
- respond to a child's attempt to assert independence as if it were rebellion. These parents clamp down with more rules and aggressive or physical discipline.
- give their children little chance to spread their wings.

Active, aggressive children will be constantly reined in by these parents' strict limits. As toddlers and as early adolescents—periods when a sense of control is vital for a child—children in these families will be allowed little autonomy and given little chance to test their wings. They may become increasingly resentful and defiant, and they will have learned few skills to calm their rage and express their feelings constructively.

It is hard for a child to learn empathy, perspective, and compassion when a parent is rigid and dogmatic. Conflicts and control battles heat up. More trouble lies ahead unless the King of the Mountain parent can change to a style of discipline that fosters understanding, empathy, respect, and mutual responsibility for resolving conflict.

"Time to clean your room, Mary Lynn," Dad called to his daughter from the bottom of the stairs. Mary Lynn poked her head out into the hallway and said, "I'm right in the middle of a really good chapter in my book. Can't I clean my room in half an hour?"

Dad's face turned red, and he rushed up the stairs, two at a time. Towering over his daughter, he shouted, "No, you can't clean it in half an hour, or even half a minute! You will clean it right now! Is that understood, young lady?"

Mary Lynn backed away and asked softly, "But why can't I just wait until I've finished my chapter, Dad?"

Her father roared, "Because I'm your father, and I say it's time to clean your room right now! Now move!" Mary Lynn scuttled back into her bedroom and obeyed her father's order.

Her father could not see her slamming her things around her room or hear her thoughts of rage.

Queen of the Worried: Frozen by Uncertainty

Jokes abound about the worry-riddled parent who sees catastrophes and calamity around every corner. Instead of admiring her three-year-old's pride at putting on her own shoes, Mom prods her daughter to come have her shoes tied before she trips. Instead of discussing values and responsible choices, Dad rigidly says, "No dating." Worried parents actively try to control every aspect of their child's life.

"Queen of the Worried" Parents:

* are often highly anxious and easily aroused. When their infant cries, they quickly become agitated, unconsciously creating more tension and arousal in their distressed baby.
* are likely to have a difficult time developing a sense of calm and a feeling of being "in sync" with their young child.
* respond with shaming, blaming, and lectures, then fail to discipline effectively.
* feel panicky about their teenager's growing independence. When the teenager makes a mistake, the Worried parent may overreact. The teenager, afraid of seeming like a failure, may resentfully withdraw.
* fail to become a resource or a sounding board for their teenagers.

Because parents tend to disguise their actions with a mask of helpfulness, the child feels that he cannot question their authority, discuss what he needs, or respond in anger. He feels he must build up the "good parent" mythology. He thinks, *It isn't right to argue with Mom or tell her I want to make more decisions for myself. She'll think she's failed me . . . or she'll just criticize and nag me harder. If I tell her how I really feel, I'll get even less freedom, so I just won't say anything.* These children learn to avoid conflict at all costs.

Children of Queen of the Worried parents may become very indirect in expressing their frustration and anger. Acts of revenge and sabotage are common. These children also run the risk of becoming martyrs or developing one or more of the following problems for their "good parent" to fix:

* phobias
* eating disorders

- difficulty with wetting or soiling
- sleep disruption
- imaginary illnesses

They cannot express their rage and resolve it directly, so they fight the struggle for control on the turf of their own bodies. These children *can* control their bodies, even if the control is destructive. Since they can never please their parents, they can become masters at disappointing them.

Teenagers can develop a very masterful way of winning against the "good" parent: going on strike. Shutting down, not showing how they feel, keeps their parents from intruding on their privacy and freedom. Withholding information gains the teenager a sense of control. Silent sulks create needed distance. A secret life will allow a teen a sense of freedom. But a vicious circle sets in. The more the parent hovers, the more the child retreats; the more the parent worries, the more the teen is enraged. Tempers explode. Walls of resentment build.

Children with a strong need for control and well-developed communication skills may learn to manipulate the anxious parent, by playing on Mom's vulnerability to criticism and failure. Instead of going on strike, they strike out. Tired of the lectures and guilt trips, they throw them back:

> *"If you don't give me my way, I won't talk to you anymore." "I want that dress, and if you don't buy it for me, I'm going to call Grandma. She knows you're a terrible mother. . . ."*

The Teacher: The Child Can Learn to Control the Dragon

"Teacher" parents offer their children information, training, and options for resolving problems. They keep a sense of humor and make learning fun. They often come up with creative solutions that give the child a sense of control. They remember that every family has conflicts and recognize that anger can promote growth and change.

"Teacher" Parents:
- act as authority figures and consultants to their children.
- have the strength to set limits and consequences for inappropriate expressions of anger.
- set examples of sensitivity, fairness, and consideration.
- encourage direct communication.
- see problems as opportunities for the family to learn.
- promote democratic discussions of solutions.
- demonstrate, by example, the value of self-control.

"Teacher" parents look for the cause of their child's anger, but they do not stop there. They work with their child and others as a team to find solutions to conflicts. If one approach doesn't work, they are flexible enough to consider other ways. They realize that the ways *they* express anger are their most powerful teaching tools.

Throughout this book, you will learn suggestions and techniques to help you develop a Teacher style of parenting. In the following example, Tom's parents learn to work together, using a Teacher style, to help their son gain self-control and to tame his Dragon of Anger.

> *Twelve-year-old Tom had always been a "difficult" boy. He had a lightning-quick fuse and would lash out—always, it seemed, at the most inappropriate times. Teachers did not appreciate his curse words; peers did not appreciate his violence. Tom's parents had learned to expect that with each new school and each new friend, they would soon get a call from a concerned parent.*
>
> *For years, Tom's parents had been odds about how to handle their son. Mom, who came from a military family, advocated a firm hand, and increasingly pushed for very strict punishments. Dad's parents had been alcoholics; he was always worried about why Tom seemed so angry. Dad believed that he and Mom had not yet gotten to the real root of Tom's problems, despite years of talking and asking Tom why he did what he did.*
>
> *Tom's parents believed they had tried everything. Now they felt stuck, frustrated and paralyzed by indecision. They worried that their son would soon turn to drugs or gangs.*

To help their son learn to control his anger, Tom's parents took the following steps:

1. *They found common ground.* Although their styles and ideas differed, Tom's parents immediately agreed on two things: (a) Tom was almost a teenager, and he had to get in control of his anger problem; and (b) Tom had no idea how to control his temper.

2. *They brought in outside help.* They met with two of Tom's teachers and spoke privately with Tom's best friend. All agreed that Tom needed to control his temper and that they were willing to help him with his problem.

3. *They made Tom a part of the team.* His parents said they realized that Tom resented the adults who were always discussing his "problems." They understood why he felt that his parents and all the other people in his life were trying to "control" him. Now, they explained calmly, Tom was going to work together with the people who cared about him to solve his anger problems.

4. *They explained, step by step, what they expected from their son and gave him as much responsibility as possible to do each step.* Tom's

first step was to arrange times to meet one-on-one with each of his parents, the two teachers, and his best friend. At each meeting, he was to get ideas about how they controlled their tempers and solved problems.

5. *They followed up at school.* Tom and his parents had a follow-up meeting with his social studies teacher and negotiated for Tom to get school credit for writing an essay on nonviolent conflict-resolution strategies. He also became part of a peer advisory group whose role was to serve as a "swat team," available in the halls and at lunch for the other junior high students to use to mediate conflicts.

6. *They used examples from their own lives to help Tom think of ways to solve anger problems—and to recognize that he would need these skills throughout his own life.* Tom's parents openly discussed the frustration they experienced each day at work, and asked Tom for advice. How could they keep from strangling their boss, who took credit for all the hard work they had just done on a project? How could Tom's dad deal with the pressure he felt from his own divorced parents to come to both of their homes for Thanksgiving?

7. *They helped Tom learn that conflicts are inevitable, but that he could gain status and success only if he learned to be "cool."* He learned new ideas about problem solving, but recognized that he still had a tough time applying many of the ideas because he had such a quick fuse. A breakthrough came when Tom asked his coach how he could cool down his anger and stay focused during competitions. His coach gave him some physical strategies that Tom gradually began to use in many situations.

8. *They established and maintained clear rules to help Tom stay in control.* Like most kids, Tom still needed the "safety net" of losing privileges and adding extra chores when he totally blew his stack. He still needed his dad to talk to him about why he was so angry. But Tom learned that he often didn't know *why* until much later.

By learning to be in control and taking charge of himself, Tom learned to control his Dragon of Anger. His temper became less fiery. Friends no longer avoided him. His parents no longer felt frustrated and paralyzed but became more confident in their new roles as teachers and models of anger control.

Test Your Parenting Style

Before you can help your child, you need new ways to deal with your own anger. The first step is a self-inventory, an assessment of your parenting style. Think about how you would respond to the following situations. (It's fine to choose more than one response.)

1. *Your three-year-old son has been cranky all day. After a horrible tantrum, you put him down for a nap. He bites you.*

a. You bite him back, saying, "See what it feels like."

b. You let it pass and rock him to sleep.

c. You worry about what might be bothering him and call someone for advice.

d. You say, "Biting is not OK. After you have a nice sleep, we will talk about what to do when you're angry."

2. *Your preteen has been avoiding chores. Every request turns into an angry tirade. She promises to have her room cleaned by the time you get home from work. You come home, and her room is messier than ever.*

a. You yell in frustration that she is grounded indefinitely.

b. You give her another chance when she explains that she just had so-o-o much homework to do.

c. You give lecture #398 about why she must learn to be more responsible and how much work you already do around the house and how much more fun you could have together if she would only get her work done before you get home.

d. You close the door and tell her that, as you had agreed, she will have no phone calls, TV, or friends over until the room is clean.

3. *Your son had a fight on the playground. When a teacher tried to break up the fight, your son slugged the teacher.*

a. You give your son the spanking of his life.

b. You believe your son when he says the other kid started it and that the teacher has a reputation for being rough and must be exaggerating.

c. You worry about your son's low self-esteem and are concerned that he might be getting a bad reputation. You cannot agree with the school staff about what to do because you aren't absolutely sure what is bothering your son.

d. You let your son know that, regardless of the cause of his anger and no matter how others may have acted, nothing justifies hitting and violence. You ask him to practice some ways he could have solved the problem, so that when he apologizes, he can explain what he will do so the fighting does not happen again.

4. *A friend was over to play and broke your daughter's special music box. Your daughter proudly told you how she refrained from giving the girl a black eye. Later you learn that your daughter has been spreading vicious rumors about the other girl.*

a. You order your daughter to go to school and to tell everyone she lied—and if she doesn't, she will really get punished.

b. You understand that your daughter must have been very hurt and try to console her.

c. You worry that your daughter's reputation may be ruined if she admits she was spreading rumors. You worry that the girls' friendship might be broken, so you try to patch things up with a slumber party.

d. You let your daughter know that it is up to her to decide how she will make amends to her friend. You practice how she can tell her friend how angry she was about the broken music box. You let her know that, until she does these things, she will have to do one hour of extra chores each day.

5. *Your son is very careful with his work, even perfectionistic at times. He has been sick. The first day back at school, he flunks a math test. He calls the teacher an [expletive deleted] and refuses to go to the principal's office when reprimanded.*

a. You tell your son he must respect authority, and you force him to apologize to the teacher immediately.

b. You understand that your son has been through a rough time and talk to him about how he must be feeling.

c. You worry that your son will not be accepted into the Honor Society and tell him he must try harder.

d. You let your son know that we all have bad days and lose it sometimes. You know he is harder on himself than anyone else could be. You give him a day to think about how he will forgive himself for blowing it and to make a plan about how he will make things right.

If you have answered mostly a's, you may be a King of the Mountain. This parenting style may make you particularly prone to attacking and coming on too strong. Your goal throughout this book will be to learn more cooperative ways to solve conflicts.

If you have answered mostly b's, you are probably an Appeaser. Be careful of excusing or indulging your child's angry tirades. Your goal will be to learn effective discipline techniques.

If you have answered mostly c's, you probably fretted with indecision over each question and wished there had been more information. If you felt paralyzed by this simple test, you may have an even more difficult time making decisions in the heat of a conflict. Your goal will be to learn to take effective action.

If you are like most of us, you probably marked a, b, and c to most of the questions! We all react differently, depending on our mood and energy level. We all wish we could pick those "d" responses; they sound so reasonable in theory. But what about in practice? In the heat of anger, it can seem impossible to stay calm and rational. Self-control becomes easier with practice! The Teacher style of learning to control anger can become second nature to you and your child.

In a two-parent family, partners need to work together to teach children constructive ways to deal with anger. Chapter 5 offers ideas for parents to work effectively as a team, even if their problem-solving styles are different.

5

Two-Parent Families

PROBLEM-SOLVING STYLES

Anger is such a difficult emotion because it demands a response. When family members get angry, everybody responds differently. In two-parent families, each partner's anger style—what you say when you're angry and how you say it—is probably different. Responses that satisfy your child may not be acceptable to your partner or to other family members. The result can be conflict, not only between you and your child, but also between you and your partner.

In the "ideal" family, both adults would share parenting responsibilities equally and provide consistency for their children. But if perfect equity is your goal, you are doomed to a sense of failure. Because in the real world, couples develop a family-centered division of labor that is not perfectly equal but, rather, is based on their interests, energies, talents, and work schedules.

The style your family uses for managing conflict and resolving problems will be a lifelong model for your child. This chapter examines the most typical styles of problem solving and conflict management within today's families. It will help you identify your own family's problem-solving style and show how you and your partner can work as a team to Tame the Dragon.

The Legacy of Family
Parenting Styles

Like stories, lore, and heirlooms, family patterns are handed down but seldom examined too closely. The patterns provide the framework for what is "normal" within a particular family. You usually become most aware of your own patterns and styles when you establish a household and try to combine two different sets of expectations. When you become parents, the patterns and compromises that may have worked for you as a couple may no longer be effective. Conflicts between parenting styles can build with the stress of children.

Let's begin with a few basic questions to consider as you read the rest of this chapter:

1. Is our family a dictatorship, a monarchy, or a democracy?
2. Do we have a routine for airing complaints and concerns?
3. Do we talk about issues that surface, or do we avoid them?
4. Do we have a sense of order, or is our decision-making process confused and chaotic?
5. Do we listen to and respect everyone's feelings?
6. Do we focus on blame for what went wrong, or do we concentrate on taking responsibility for what will go right next time?

Five Typical Problem-Solving Styles

Next let's look at five typical styles of problem solving within two-parent families and examine the limitations and strengths of each.

Avoid It: The Dragon Is a Secret

Although conflict is normal, to some parents it can be terrifying. Avoid the problem. Don't see it. Procrastinate. Ignore your feelings.

Parents who use the "Avoid It" style do little to help their children learn to recognize and accept their own feelings. How, then, can children understand the feelings and needs of others?

This style does not teach children the crucial skills of negotiation and compromise. The family is too busy pretending that nothing is wrong. Children from Avoid It families learn to deal with the stresses and strains of human relationships only when someone outside the family shows them how. The following example illustrates how problems can escalate in Avoid It Style families.

Mary's family had been abusive, and its conflicts destructive and divisive. Ken's family had been of the free-spirit, free-expression variety,

*where everything was fair game; family members especially tried to
see how many people they could manipulate to be on their side of
an argument. When Mary and Ken got married, both vowed never to
repeat the mistakes of the past. They froze in fear when any disagreement surfaced, and they worked hard to bury their anger and
"get back to normal."*

*After their twins were born, their lives turned upside down. The
pressures were enormous, and conflicts were everywhere, but neither
Mary nor Ken wanted to face them.*

*Billy was the easy twin. Anything his parents did seemed to work.
Mandy was the challenge. Constantly on the move, she yelled, kicked,
and bit to get her way. So she got her way.*

*Mary and Ken could never agree on what to do, and Mandy's
rages escalated. As she grew older, the calls and complaints from
other parents became more frequent. Her parents found themselves
numb. They didn't want to face the problem. They found it easier to
doubt what others were telling them: that Mandy was out of control.*

*Mandy's parents tried changing schools, finding new friends for
her, even counseling. But they resented the counselor's insinuation
that they needed to look at their own ways of solving problems before
they could help Mandy. The situation seemed so overwhelming that
they just did nothing, and hoped that Mandy would simply grow out
of it.*

Attack: Let's Slay the Dragon

Rising pressures. Explosive rage. Overflowing emotions. Uncontrollable
tempers.

Conflict can escalate quickly to the danger zone when "Attack"
seems the only solution. The family that uses the Attack style is constantly
on the verge of crisis. Parents who use the Attack style may set no boundaries on their anger, and no limits to what people may say or do when
the Dragon roars. The family's members experience hurt and, in turn,
they hurt others.

Children who live in Attack-style families are likely to feel so
wounded, angry, hurt, and resentful that revenge often seems the only
way to resolve conflict. Their parents should not be surprised when their
children begin to retaliate against them.

*Brett was a challenge. Never easy to manage, he resented his parents'
authority. Even when his dad came down hard with a swift punishment, Brett never seemed to learn. Now that he was starting high
school, he was no longer just a bully; he was showing signs of getting
involved with gangs. The tougher Brett acted, the harder his parents
tried to clamp down.*

Brett's angry flare-ups threatened to become physical confrontations at home. He was already bigger than his mother and had hit her this week. His dad had pulled the door off its hinges and chased Brett as he ran out of the house, defying the six-month grounding his father had imposed.

As Brett's parents became more frustrated and more frightened for his welfare, they became more strict and rigid. They believed they had no option except overpowering their out-of-control son. They firmly believed that the only way to deal with their son's Dragon was to attack and slay. They did not realize that all Brett was learning from them was violence and more anger.

Divide and Conquer: Recruit the Dragon

Isn't it the kids who try to divide and conquer, usually with transparent methods? *"But* Mom *said I could go to the game. Why are* you *being so mean?"*

Adults, too, use this conflict-management approach, with more destructive results. Divide and Conquer style parents spoil, overindulge, and fail to set limits on their children's angry outbursts. They allow a child to rage against the other parent, or a brother or sister, particularly if the parent is angry at that person, too.

In families that use this style, a parent can unknowingly foster a child's dependency and loyalty, so that the child sides with the parent in "wars" against other family members. This may give both the parent and child a sense of power, but it is ultimately destructive to the family.

Dividing and conquering is about power and control. Subversive tactics—cold shoulders, sarcasm, emotional distancing, and other forms of rejection—can be powerful weapons in the anger wars. But this style does not allow families to settle differences, and solve problems. Feuds never end. Animosities fester, and wars erupt over minor territorial issues. The Dragon of Anger can seem unstoppable.

Paralyzed by Fear and Worry: Analyze the Dragon

Nothing escapes this family. In this style, the family members examine, reexamine, and study everything for meaning, including feelings. They analyze and reanalyze differences, compulsively searching for the *why*. They will explore and reexplore issues, expecting that deep resolution will occur.

In the "Paralyzed" family's endless search through the trees, they lose the forest. They rarely decide on an actual resolution plan as they consider any attempts at preventing future conflicts as shallow—unless everyone first fully understands why the original conflict happened.

Children in these families may develop elaborate thinking patterns
for examining emotions, but they often have few skills to resolve conflicts
or to prevent problems from recurring. The following shows what can
happen in a family that uses this approach to solving problems.

> *Dylan was creative, a gifted student and a talented artist. Sensitive
> and hardworking, he often seemed driven by some internal pressure
> to be the best at everything. He became overwhelmed when anyone
> criticized him or when his work turned out less than perfect. He would
> brood and storm for hours, punishing himself with extra work and
> projects. He expected perfection from his parents as well.*
>
> *Dylan's parents only made things worse. Their obsessive worry
> when he seemed upset put more pressure on their son. Their constant
> questions about what was bothering him only made Dylan more self-
> absorbed and more self-destructive. When they tried to talk to him,
> they could not hide their tremendous anxiety that something was
> deeply wrong. Their worry fueled Dylan's own self-doubts. He became
> increasingly angry when he and others made even minor mistakes.*
>
> *The crisis hit when Dylan's school counselor called to say that
> Dylan had slashed the tires of his calculus teacher's new sports car.
> Dylan came home and locked himself in his room, refusing to talk to
> his parents about what was bothering him. He would not come down
> for meals and became totally obsessed with his Dungeons and Drag-
> ons game. His parents felt paralyzed, and blamed themselves so
> much that they had no energy left to find a solution.*

If your family is paralyzed by fear and rage, there is hope. You do
not need to go deeper into why you have a problem and who is at fault.
Too much of this is extremely counterproductive. Rather, your family
needs to lighten up. You need to focus on your strengths and use your
creativity and energy to find new solutions. You need to gather your
courage to face the Dragon of Anger. When you stop seeing conflict as
failure, you can begin to see conflict for what it is: motivation, opportunity for change, and energy for solutions.

Opportunity for Change:
Teach the Dragon to Be in Control

Conflict and anger do not have to lead to destructive and divisive habits.
You can use the energy anger brings as a motivator for change. You can
replace blame with personal responsibility. Attacks can become assertive
expressions of need. Warring sides can call a truce and work as a team.

Once you learn to see the old patterns, you can stop them. You can
then focus your energies on becoming a teacher. You can use the skills

that follow in later chapters to be an effective problem solver, communicator, and, when needed, disciplinarian—all in the spirit of teaching your child to handle anger effectively and responsibly.

What Is Your Family's Problem-Solving Style?

To discover your family's style of solving problems and managing conflict, observe your family, and yourself, during the next week. As you observe, pay particular attention to who does what. Which of the preceding styles most closely characterizes your family? The following questions will help you focus your observations:

1. Who most often displays anger?
2. Do displays of anger create problems or seem appropriate to the situation?
3. Who is quickest to respond?
4. Who promotes and encourages discussion?
5. Who avoids conflict and discussion?
6. Who attacks?
7. Who is overly responsible?
8. Who decides what the problem is, and how are these decisions made?
9. Who has a say in what to do about the problem?
10. Whose say wins?
11. If one family member is absent, how does this change the pattern?
12. If competing patterns and styles exist, do they coincide peacefully or provide opportunities for further conflict?

By answering these questions and tracking your own and your family's patterns of anger expression, conflict management, and discipline, you are becoming more aware of your family's strengths and weaknesses. You will know where to focus your energies for change within yourself before expecting changes in your child. The techniques discussed in the rest of this book will require you first to be motivated to *change your own patterns*.

Combining Different Syles

Teamwork in parenting requires respect for each other's preferences, needs, desires and styles. Consistency in using one problem-solving style may not be a reasonable goal for you, because you and your partner probably brought unique and quite different emotional style into your relationship. For example, what if your partner wants perfect quiet during the evenings, and you allow rowdy, rough-and-tumble play? No problem. Children can adapt to differing personalities and routines, as long as the expectations are clear.

But what if parents have widely varying styles of anger expression and conflict management? One of you may tend to avoid conflict, yet have a strong need for long, deep "feeling" discussions. The other may be easily aroused, quick to respond with words and gestures, and just as quick to forget the issue. Again, there is no single right way. It is more important that your children see a complementary balance and a respect for each other's problem-solving style. Of course, verbal or physical abuse is never appropriate for you or your children. You must identify destructive patterns, then find ways to change them. The more anger-management styles and techniques that children can learn and use to cope positively with conflict, the more equipped they will be for dealing with the real world.

Assessing the Effectiveness of Different Problem-Solving Styles

Keeping a Log

If you and your partner have different styles, you can use a simple log, or running list, to observe and record how each of your children responds to your styles. The log will help you recognize which of your anger-management styles is most effective with each of your children. It will become a written reminder of the ways your family expresses anger productively and problem-solves and will help you pinpoint the areas that need attention.

Keep the log's format simple. (The more complex you make it, the less useful it will be and the less likely you'll be to stick with it.) Following is an easy format for setting up your log:

1. Write each family member's name across the top of the page.

2. Down the left side, write Problem 1, 2, 3, 4, etcetera. Leave room to write a brief word or phrase describing the problem.

3. When an anger-related problem occurs, log under each person's name and what styles he or she used to try to solve the conflict. Avoid it? Divide and conquer? Attack and slay? Paralyzed by worry? Or teaching—using the problem as a learning opportunity to prevent future conflicts?

4. Keep your log for a week, then review it with your partner. (If

each of you is keeping a separate log, you may have very different versions of the same events! That's OK. It's important for each of you to keep an open mind as you compare notes.)

5. As you review your log, be careful not to place blame. Simply try to agree on how members of your family usually express anger and how conflict typically builds.

6. Try to identify which anger styles each family member uses most often. Which styles fuel the anger; which promote soothing and healing? Which styles work best for individual family members?

After reviewing your log, you then have an important decision to make: Should both of you try to incorporate a style that is compatible with your child's healthy anger expression, or should one of you temporarily assume more responsibility for anger control, conflict management, and discipline of that child?

Remember, there is no right answer to this question. The solution depends on your own family, your energy and priorities, and on the current goals you have for your child.

What If You Can't Agree on One Style?

Maybe parents cannot agree on the best style to use for a child. For example, you may believe that your partner's active, verbal barrage of anger is compounding your child's difficulties. Or your partner may believe that *your* style—worrying and holding back on issues—is the problem. Major differences of opinion such as these indicate that you and your partner have not resolved your own differences in style.

Talk to Each Other

Although resentments and frustrations may surface, don't panic. You are not bad parents. Discuss your differences and negotiate ways to balance your styles. Try new anger-management strategies, discussed in later chapters, which may be helpful for your child and may be a departure from each of your styles.

Support Each Other

Beware: Children are quite skillful at finding their parents' points of vulnerability. The divide-and-conquer approach often works. Children who can split their parents can distract attention from their own misbehavior or inappropriate anger outbursts. Be observant. If this is happening to you as parents, it still does not mean that you must be totally consistent or totally in agreement. It *does* mean that you must *support* each other.

•*Be prepared to support your partner's interventions (nonviolent, of course), even if you would have handled the situation differently.* Later, away from your child, you can discuss how you might handle a similar situation in the future.

•*Focus on the styles of anger expression and conflict resolution that you want to provide your child.* Your goal should be meeting your child's needs and respecting both parents' styles.

•*If you can't reach a compromise on parenting issues, you must shield your child from destructive, irresolvable conflicts.* In this situation, you must make a choice: Does one partner take primary responsibility for all parenting? Or do you enter couple's or family counseling to resolve these issues?

Get Professional Help

Therapy is indicated if you are replaying old problems from before when your child was born, or if your child is quite young. If your child is age eight or older, it is likely that he or she is playing a key role in maintaining your parenting conflicts. If so, family counseling is needed. In family sessions, you will have time to focus on the parenting team and to develop a balanced anger-management style. Your child will learn how to stop destructive, divisive tactics and create new ways to express anger and manage conflict.

The next chapter offers suggestions for coping with the special pressures and stresses of single-parent families.

6

The Single-Parent Family

Going it alone is tough. Single parents have all the parenting responsibilities; it's difficult ever to get a break. Time, money, even fun with the kids—all seem to be in short supply. The demands can seem overwhelming; the stress unbelievable. Resentments build, and it's easy to become short-tempered with children. The Dragon of Anger is primed to explode when everyone feels so overwhelmed and frustrated.

Ways to Cope with Single-Parenting Pressures

As a single parent, you may be spending most of your energy on the physical demands of caring for your child, your job, and your house. You may feel that you have little left for your child's emotional caretaking, let alone for the most important caretaking of all—yours. When under stress, you need to change your priorities. Following are some suggestions for how to cope.

1. *Find time to play with your child.* As you do, you will find yourself rejuvenated and less quick to flare up. When children have time with their parents to play and laugh, they will have less need to draw attention in negative ways. The nurturing power of play, hugs, and humor is your most important tool in Taming the Dragon of Anger.

2. *Find relief.* Develop a support base within your neighborhood, your child's school, or your office, or from another source such as with friend or relatives. Let other, trusted adults care for your child at times. Then use the time to do something for yourself. Do not feel guilty or tell

yourself you are "dumping" your child. You need the break, and your child will benefit from the exposure to others.

   3. *Allow a buffer time for your child to decompress whenever he or she has been away.* A quiet time to relax or just "veg out" is essential to lessen the stress of reentry and to make time away truly a break for each of you. Try not to rush into the house and tackle the endless chores. Dishes can wait; kids can't. Allow time to nurture and reconnect.

   4. *If you are divorced, use your ex-partner as much as possible for child care.* Even if you have widely differing styles, your child can adapt to two families. Be businesslike and cordial with your ex, so that you do not place further stress on your child by exposing him or her to your differences or conflicts.

   5. *If divorced, work as a team with your ex.* Share information. Do not let myths and prejudices build. Talk to each other about how you each deal with your child's anger. Getting the complete picture and hearing all sides can prevent "divide and conquer" schemes from developing into a war. Be respectful. Listen and problem-solve with your ex-partner in front of your child. If tempers flare, take a break and set a time later to talk in private about how you will work together to parent your angry child.

The Divorced Family

Some single parents and their children are coping with a divorce. The period from separation to one year after the divorce is extremely stressful. Sane, rational adults can feel and even act insane and do some highly irrational things. Anger is raw, overflowing, and at times explosive. Children sense their parents' vulnerability and may try to become temporary protectors and caretakers. They may minimize and deny their own feelings so that their parents do not have to worry about them.

Helping Children Accept the Divorce

At first most children do not fully believe their parents' explanation that the divorce will be better for the family in the long run and will make Mom and Dad happier. How could they? All they may see is loss, hurt, anger, and misery. They may see adults who are often too preoccupied with their own problems to attend to their children's needs.

   Children are afraid to express their fears about loss. "If you stopped loving Daddy/Mommy, will you stop loving me?" Many children are exposed to tension and conflict whenever their parents meet. They see the power of anger and are at once intimidated and inspired. They know anger gets results. Hurt and lost, some children become increasingly defiant and aggressive, knowing their parents cannot work together to respond. By being out of control with their feelings, these children are gaining much-needed attention. They hope their parents will realize how out of control, hurt, and angry they feel.

The following example shows how a divorced couple helped their child move constructively toward accepting a divorce.

> *Despite both parents' efforts to have a civilized divorce and always to place their daughter's needs first, Melissa seemed very angry. She became especially uncontrollable immediately before and after each visit to her dad's. Stormy, demanding, resentful, and downright hateful, Melissa had gotten so difficult that her mother was having trouble controlling her own temper.*
>
> *Mom had anticipated that Melissa would use "divide-and-conquer" strategies, but she was not prepared for how divisive these could be. For example, Melissa told Mom that Dad never fed her on Sundays before he took her back to Mom. She told Dad that Mom swatted her with a hairbrush.*
>
> *If her parents had not been talking regularly together, they might have believed some of their daughter's claims. Mom knew Melissa was hurting, but this was no excuse for her rampages. How could she help Melissa to get back her sense of humor and her sense of hope?*

Melissa needed creative ideas for how she could grieve for the family she would never again have. She and her mom needed to invent new ways of being together, feeling close, and having fun. Melissa's mother used a "Teacher" parenting style in the following ways to help her daughter control her anger and accept the changes in her life.

1. *She continued to reassure Melissa that both parents would always love her, even though they were happier apart.*

2. *She made a special effort to be civil to Melissa's dad and to work cooperatively with him to help their daughter find a safe outlet for her anger.* For Melissa, the outlet was a gymnastics course, where she could release physical tension, make new friends, and feel successful at her new activity.

3. *By trial and error, Melissa's mom found new ways to talk to her daughter and to teach her to cope with the stress of change and the loss of divorce.* By showing how she had done her grieving and healed her own anger, Mom taught Melissa ways to move forward.

Consider how Melissa's problems might have escalated if her mother had not used a "Teacher" style:

- A "King of the Mountain" might have severely punished Melissa, making her feel more resentful and misunderstood, and even angrier that no one really cared about her needs.
- A "Queen of the Worried" might have been so obsessed with

protecting Melissa that the mother may have become suspicious and mistrustful of Melissa's father. Then a cycle of blame and misunderstanding could have built into major conflicts between the parents, putting further pressure on Melissa.

- An "Appeaser" might simply have excused Melissa's angry tirades as caused by the divorce. Paralyzed by worry and afraid of stifling Melissa's legitimate anger, the "Appeaser" might have done nothing. Melissa would have felt even more abandoned and insecure without the safety net of parental control.

Children do not need explosive eruptions between their parents at each visitation exchange. They do not need divide-and-conquer tactics. Being forced to take sides will frighten and anger them, regardless of the fleeting rush of power they may feel at aligning with the "winning" parent. Children do not need to keep secrets and to be forced to hide their anger. They *do* need permission to feel angry and to be understood.

Children need their parents to heal themselves and return to their positions of caretakers, nurturers, and decision-makers. They need to see the end of revenge and feuds, the end of mistrust and blame, and the beginning of a climate of mutual respect.

When to Seek Professional Help

If your family situation has not stabilized one year after a divorce, you may need professional help. The hurt and loss may be too intense, too frequently expressed in anger, and too divisive. A professional evaluation can assess what issues may be contributing to a lack of healing and how your family can address these issues.

Death of a Parent

Shock. Denial. Pain. Anger. Acceptance. These are the stages of grief that you and your child must pass through after the devastating loss of a partner and parent. No one could expect each of you to have these feelings in the same order for the same length of time. You and your child may feel misunderstood and alone when different feelings emerge all at once. Frustration can build and conflict erupt. Everyone needs support and comfort.

Yet, the tension-reducing methods that used to work well for your family (humor, play, sporting events) may seem inappropriate after a death. Formerly effective styles of conflict resolution may break down, particularly if the parent who has died was instrumental in bringing everyone together. Instead of rallying and growing closer, your family may feel on the verge of destruction.

If your child appears stuck in the angry phase of grieving, you must look at your capacity to respond. How much nurturing, support, and understanding can you provide right now? Especially if you are being attacked and are feeling the brunt of your child's rage? Ask these questions:

- Why is my child stuck in the angry phase?
- How am I contributing to the problem? Is my child likely to hurt himself or herself or others?
- Should I be encouraging appropriate anger expression now or focusing more on the loss and pain, or both?
- Is a period of avoidance (ignoring the angry outbursts) appropriate as a short-term respite?
- What other things can I do to relieve the emotional pressure on my child?

When to Seek Professional Help

If you are far enough in your own healing, begin with the techniques in this book to help your child. If you feel weak, wounded, and unable to respond to your child's anger, look for a professional therapist or other adult with experience in death-related issues to assess your child.

What to Do When You're Wondering "Why?"

Many parents believe, "If only I could figure out *why* my child gets so angry, then I would know what to do." The answer to *Why?* is important, but never simple. There are usually many reasons why you and your child lose your tempers. When you both feel the pressure building at the same time, the risk of explosion is very high. First you need to put out the fire; then you can investigate the causes.

It's normal for angry outbursts to happen more often during times of family crisis such as a divorce. But they're never easy to cope with, especially when you're struggling to control the destructive side of your own anger and to teach your child responsible coping skills. When your child explodes, you may feel paralyzed, frustrated, guilty—and nearly as angry as your child. *What do I do to calm her down? Is it my fault she's acting this way? Should I send her to her father? Am I the only parent in the world who can't control her child? Why won't she STOP IT? Why didn't an instruction manual come with this kid?*

The most important thing for you to do, as you continue reading this book, is to be aware of how you affect your child. You must recognize the example and model you are providing for how your child will express anger. You must recognize what types of anger expression you are reinforcing, knowingly and unwittingly, in your child. Then you can become effective at helping your child. By mastering the interventions and techniques that follow, you can successfully change yourself and your child.

Think of the many times when you and your child have dealt with angry feelings that erupted as you both struggled to cope with change and loss. Focus on what went right during the transition. Remember when a sense of humor, compassion, and understanding helped dissolve the tension that change creates. Think about how you achieved peace by waiting until you and your child were calm, then hearing each other talk about what to do to stop the hurtful anger and move forward together. Build from positive solutions and new skills you are discovering in yourself. Incorporate the ideas in this book into your unique bag of tricks for Taming the Angry Dragon.

7

When Parents Need Help

If your family has experienced or is in the midst of significant stress, you know the feeling of being overwhelmed and out of control. The demands of changing yourself, let alone your child, may seem impossible.

You need professional help if you and your family have been facing either of the following issues for more than one year *and* if you are experiencing intense anger or conflicts. The suggestions and advice discussed in this book can be effective, but they will not be enough.

Substance Abuse and Alcoholism

An addict or alcoholic virtually ensures a breakdown in the family's ability to communicate feelings. Conflict-management styles tend to swing widely between avoidance and explosive rages. Children are taught not to feel and to ignore the warning signs of stress and tension within their own minds and bodies. Nevertheless, an undercurrent of turmoil and rage flows, at first blocked and later bursting.

Family members cannot learn effective ways to solve problems or manage conflict in this situation. Instead, they desperately practice avoidance: *The Dragon is a secret. What problem?*

Then comes the battle. Addicted or alcoholic parents either will absolve themselves of all responsibility *or* take too much responsibility, in a martyrlike fashion, begging for forgiveness. No resolution occurs. Tensions build, and everyone escapes: the addict, through drink or drug; the family, by becoming numb.

Children from these families often express their frustration and anger outside the family. Socially, they often do poorly because they have few skills in expressing feelings or resolving conflicts. Emotionally, with their peers, they tend to overreact to hurt, loss, or criticism. They may be masters at blame, ridiculing themselves or deflecting all responsibility onto others. Already on edge, they may turn minor provocations into temper outbursts. If a teacher calls their parents, this expression of public concern becomes one more family pressure, another opportunity to follow the pattern of avoidance, blame, and explosion.

Steps toward Change

If you are an addict or alcoholic, or your partner is, wake up! You need to:

1. Realize the difficulties your addiction or alcoholism is creating for your child.

2. Understand that your child's tantrums and deficient social skills are not the main problem—the addiction or substance abuse is.

3. Take full responsibility for having a substance abuse problem. Do not minimize, blame, or shift the responsibility. For example, do not try to place the responsibility onto school staff and push them to handle it because "it only happens in school." Take control of your life.

4. Treat the addiction or alcoholism and the co-dependency.

5. Apologize to your child.

6. Recognize that these changes will be vital for your child's emotional well-being.

Do not be surprised if, just when your addiction problem is under control, your child seems *more* angry, rebellious, or defiant. It is a sign of progress that your child can share his or her feelings at home, even in an inappropriate way. Tell your child that all of your family can learn together how to express and deal with feelings effectively. Then you are ready for this book.

The Abusive Parent

Abusive parents tend to follow a pattern: first avoiding conflict, then exploding, then retreating guiltily. They may be overwhelmed with a profound sense of guilt and self-recrimination, a phase that often triggers intense anger outbursts. These parents often can release tension, guilt, and anger only by taking it out on their children.

Paralyzed by worry, they may purposely avoid discipline situations for fear of lashing out. By avoiding the conflict, they may fail to set appropriate limits for their children's safety. At other times, afraid that things are falling apart, the "King of the Mountain" may step in with aggressive, sometimes violent tactics to establish rigid control at any cost.

The children of abusive parents may become unruly. Some days, the parents may not care. Other days, they may be tense and will over-react to the child's misbehavior. Abusive parents will yell and strike out. They will hurt with words and actions. Because they feel wounded themselves, some abusive parents can recognize the pain in their children's eyes. Over the years, they begin to see more: their children's anger, resentment, and desire for revenge.

Many abused children become progressively aggressive, first with siblings, then toward adults. The abusive parent's worst fear has come true. *The child has become like the parent: depressed, angry, ashamed, hurting, and looking for someone to blame.*

Steps toward Change

If this sounds like you or your partner, take action!

1. *Call for help immediately.* Don't let your shame keep you from facing the problem. You can heal yourself and your child!

2. Call your local psychological association and ask for a therapist who specializes in treating abusive parents.

3. Call Parents Anonymous (1-800-345-5044) to get help for you as well as your child. A support group and family counseling can help.

4. Once you have *established a climate of safety*, then you can use this book. You will be ready to develop the skills for empathy, open sharing of feelings, positive discipline, and effective problem solving. Your child will thank you and admire your courage.

Part II of this book, "As the Dragon Grows," will help you identify and understand your child's basic temperament and provide a chronological guide to coping with typical anger problems in preschoolers, school-age children, and teens.

PART II

AS THE DRAGON GROWS

8

Understanding Your Child's Temperament

Some children can be so easy. Haven't we all envied parents who brag about their "good baby," who sleeps through the night, regularly follows a schedule, and already is learning to console himself? Other children can be such a challenge: never settling into any routine, fussy about any change, seemingly unresponsive to any of the ways we try to soothe them. Some toddlers seem shot from a cannon, bursting with energy and never stopping.

All children are different. Each child's unique physical and emotional makeup is a far more powerful influence on anger than the child's gender. When you understand your child's developmental needs and your child's rhythms and emotions, you can prevent many angry blowups.

The Elements of Temperament

This chapter will help you identify your child's personality and style, which together are known as *temperament*. Understanding your child's temperament will help you to predict typical tensions, prevent tantrums, and help your child learn healthy ways to express frustration and anger through each of the developmental stages of childhood.

Children's temperament is strongly related to their biological makeup and will remain relatively stable throughout their lives. In 1986, psychologists Stella Chess and Alexander Thomas identified the following nine elements of temperament, which can be helpful in understanding your young child's emotional development:

1. *Activity Level.* Children vary from being calm and quiet to very busy and quick-moving.

2. *Approach-Withdrawal.* Some children are extremely outgoing, sociable, and excited by new surroundings and new challenges. Others react strongly to change; they may withdraw from a new situation rather than face the stress it produces.

3. *Regularity.* Some young children easily achieve a rhythm and routine for sleep, eating, and daily activities; others never seem able to keep predictable or regular schedules.

4. *Adaptability.* When their routines and expected activities change, some children adapt easily and readily. Others strongly resist change, through agitation or withdrawal.

5. *Physical Sensitivity.* Some young children are keenly sensitive to such stimuli as noise, temperature, taste, and touch and may feel upset and disrupted when faced with new sensations. Other children are relatively insensitive and may not react as strongly to the sensory world around them.

6. *Intensity of Reaction.* Some preschoolers are easygoing, with mild reactions to their own emotions. Other young children show intense reactions with their facial expressions, body language, and tones of voice. The intensity and vigorousness of their reactions are biologically based. Many of these children have difficulty controlling or modulating their reactions.

7. *Distractibility.* Some children are driven and focused. They can concentrate for long periods on one task—sorting blocks, for example—or spend a long time repeating an activity that interests or satisfies them. Other children can be easily distracted, losing concentration quickly or being overwhelmed by whatever is happening around them.

8. *Positive or Negative Mood.* Some preschoolers seem chronically apathetic and depressed; they often act "blue" and can't seem to rally any positive reaction. Other children can be overwhelmingly positive in their sunny dispositions, regardless of stress or conditions around them.

9. *Persistence.* Some young children have remarkably short attention spans and will quickly forget a goal or activity. Other children are extremely persistent, coming back to activities even when they were distracted from them or unable to finish.

What Is Your Child's Temperament?

Although no child can be neatly categorized into a "type," it helps to understand your child's temperamental style. As you become more sensitive to your child's unique ways of reacting to people and changes, you become better able to prevent frustrations and stresses from building into angry explosions. You become better able to respond to and soothe your child, to discuss conflicts, and to use discipline in ways that are best for your child's unique style.

Let's follow four children with four different temperaments as they move through the stages of physical and emotional development. Let's see what triggers their rages. Each child has different struggles with the Dragon and issues to master to achieve a sense of control and competence.

The "Easy" Child

Your child may have an "easy" temperament: calm, unexcitable, open to new experience, and sociable, with a long attention span and a slow anger fuse. Adaptable and flexible, these children usually can adjust easily to new situations. They seldom act frustrated, overaroused, or agitated. As they grow older, they become aware of and sensitive to others' needs and can learn to control their own emotions and behavior with relatively few problems.

> *An easy temperament helps Paul adapt to body discomforts, stress, pain, and hunger. He seems to have an internal clock and thermometer that allows him to soothe himself easily. Balance comes easily for Paul, so that frustrations and hurts do not quickly explode into rage. He welcomes adult comforting, but his own remarkable ability to soothe himself helps him easily master his body.*

The ability of easy children to master their physical reactions leads then to success at the first important developmental milestone: moving from dependence to independence.

To determine whether your child has an "easy" temperament, ask yourself these questions:

- Without much personal effort, does he seem to set his own rhythms and routines?
- When changes and stresses occur, does she seem to be able to take most of them in stride?
- Is he relatively slow to be frustrated, and easily soothed and satisfied?
- Does she seem to have a sense of inner calm and focus?

If you have answered "Yes" to most of these questions, you are in luck! Intense flare-ups may be few and quickly settled. In a stress-free environment, the easy child will eagerly learn to master his moods and feelings. Your child will be receptive and will want to respond to your attempts to tame her anger. Dragon rages are unsettling, and easy children will instinctively want to return to a state of peace and calm.

The "Difficult" Child

Some young children are oversensitive and "difficult"; they tend to overreact to stress and may be hard to console. Their physical makeup makes them sensitive to tension, easily irritated, and easily frustrated. Rather than enjoying and adapting easily to new routines and new people, they may lash out and rebel. As they grow older, they may have difficulty responding to or considering the needs of others. Teaching these children to control their own impulses and learn problem-solving techniques will be a special challenge.

> *Jackie, a difficult child by nature, never seems to be able to soothe herself. Every noise, stress, change in routine, hunger signal, or other discomfort seems to set off a new wave of distress. If an adult steps in to help, Jackie seems more frustrated. She rarely acts calm, comfortable, or happy. She has such a hard time controlling her physical reactions to the world around her that she never feels in control. When frustrated, in pain, or under stress, Jackie often wails. Her rages seem never-ending.*

Difficult toddlers often remain dependent because they don't know how to soothe themselves, yet they find it hard to trust that adults can help and soothe them. Resentments and frustrations build as these children struggle to control their bodies and their emotions. They may become afraid that they can never "do it all by myself" and may resent and resist adults' attempts to help—all of which makes them still angrier. They may constantly seem irritable and oppositional.

As a parent, you already have sensed the difficult challenges some children present. To determine whether your child has a "difficult" temperament ask yourself these questions:

- Do the normal stresses, strains, and changes of the day seem to overwhelm her?
- Does he react intensely and seem overly sensitive to everything?
- Do anxieties and irritations build and escalate dramatically?
- Does she seem to stay keyed up and intensely focused on what went wrong?
- Does he have a hard time letting go, moving on and focusing on the positive?

Your child is difficult if you answered "Yes" to most of these questions. You are well aware that your home is often stormy. No matter how you try to protect your child from stress and how you plan to prevent anxieties, violent eruptions occur. Your difficult child may simmer and stew, boil over, and keep turning up the pot. Unable to regulate herself, she keeps turning up the heat of conflict.

Take heart! Of all the child types, difficult children are most responsive to the techniques described in this book. Their resistance and confrontations will be high, because the difficult child wants to be in control of everything. Change is threatening—another stress. But the techniques you will learn will provide a positive structure so that your difficult child can control his or her own stress to Tame the Dragon.

The "Active" Child

"Active" children are constantly in high gear. Busy, unsettled, distractible, and impulsive, they often have a difficult time quieting themselves and controlling their own behavior. Establishing any routine and predictability can be a challenge for their parents. Helping this type of child remain calm, even with your direction and soothing, can seem impossible. Active children's frustration tolerance is poor, and they never seem to be satisfied. Temper outbursts are frequent and intense, although they may end quickly. Other people, however, may not forget these tantrums as quickly. As they grow, active children may be considered "insensitive" or inattentive to others' feelings.

> *Ben is constantly in high gear. Busy and unsettled, he is often annoying to adults who simply cannot keep up with him. If he were just busy, Ben would be manageable, but he is often impulsive and tends to jump into the middle of everything. Adults and other children resent that he never stops to think about their feelings. Ben quickly becomes overstimulated and often seems on the verge of exhaustion, but he is too wound up to fall asleep or calm down.*

Active children often become frustrated by trying to do too much too soon. Their bodies may be zooming ahead, but their minds and their ability to communicate with others are far behind. The result is that they seem out of sync with nearly everyone. They push for independence long before they can handle themselves and quickly become frustrated when others try to apply the brakes. Their rages can be frequent and intense but end quickly, as they charge ahead to something new.

Active children keep running up against the boundaries and limits that adults set as safety nets. Instead of feeling comforted by this protection, these children often explode in resentful rages. An active preschooler may remain aloof and at an emotional distance from the other children because he has a hard time slowing down to the others' pace. The other children may resent his need to be first, and push him away.

This rejection leaves the active child still searching for a sense of closeness and security.

It is easy to know whether you have an active child. To determine whether your child has an "active" temperament, just ask yourself these questions:

- Is he always ten steps ahead of everyone else?
- When she has to slow down, do frustrations and rages erupt?
- Does he have a tough time focusing on your attempts to soothe him and to teach him to calm himself?
- Even when she knows what the rules are, what to do to stay calm, and what the consequences will be for being out of control, does she seem to break the rules or "act out" anyway?
- Is he forging ahead excitedly to new activities while others are still reeling from and angry about his latest outburst?
- Does she care, but often seem oblivious and unable to focus on the rights and feelings of others?

If your answers are mostly "Yes," you know you have a challenge with your active child. Although these children may quickly learn anger-control strategies, they often have trouble focusing and following through. They need reining in, monitoring, and prompting to be in control, but they often resent the intrusions as criticism.

Your goal will be as a coach: to provide positive rules, to keep things moving toward the goal, and to encourage mastery. Your energy can harness the enthusiasm of the active child and channel him or her toward self-control.

The "Slow-to-Warm-Up" Child

These children have great difficulty dealing with new situations and may react with anxiety, uneasiness, withdrawal, and disruptive behavior. If they can go at their own pace, they eventually will adjust to new foods, new routines, and new playmates. Parents may be surprised at how these children may focus so intensely on what was once foreboding but is now so easily mastered that they can't shift to something new. But if a parent tries to push them too quickly or expects too much too soon, "slow-to-warm-up" children may react through temper tantrums, refusing food, power struggles, or extreme fear.

> Kristy is afraid of unfamiliar people. She would rather hide in the protection of her room than come downstairs to play with visiting cousins. If her parents encourage her to "meet the nice children," she can be very stubborn, refusing to talk or even to look at the intruders. When she was a baby, it seemed to take Kristy forever to give up

her bottle. Later, she was the last in her preschool to walk willingly into her classroom, or to try out the new swing set in the play yard.

In junior high she could focus for hours on a project but had tremendous difficulty changing classes every forty minutes. Kristy seldom showed emotion, but when pushed to meet a deadline or try something different, her anger became explosive.

Slow-to-warm-up children often withdraw into themselves, are prone to tantrums when faced with new situations, and engage in power struggles over who is in control of the pace. These children are often emotionally overstimulated and overwhelmed and have a difficult time learning to soothe themselves. Rather than rushing ahead like active children, however, they prefer a slower pace and welcome a wall of protection from the outside world.

Their parents face a dilemma: Pushing these children triggers an explosion of rage; yet not to push them seems risky. If they do not master new skills as toddlers, how will they ever become independent? If they don't feel in control of their own bodies and emotions, won't they just feel even angrier?

To determine whether your child has a "slow-to-warm-up" temperament, ask yourself these questions:

- When anything new occurs, does he seem shy, resistant, and watchful?
- With old, comfortable routines, does she seem calm and intensely involved with her own internal agenda?
- Does he often seem to tune out and be oblivious to the needs of others?
- If you try to push and encourage, does she feel forced and resist?
- Although slow to anger, does he seem to hold on to resentments and frustrations much too long?

Once these children learn any new skills, particularly the anger-control techniques in this book, they will be comfortable in using them. The difficulty, however, lies in getting them to try something new. How do you push and encourage without overwhelming and frustrating? How do you build confidence in their ability to master new skills?

Fortunately, slow-to-warm-up children want to listen and to succeed, unless there has been too much force, criticism, and pressure in the past. You will learn how to push gently and to encourage positively, as you both learn to master the fears and hesitancies that fuel your child's Dragon of Anger.

Are You and Your Child
"In Sync"?

Most parents are sensitive enough to their children's personalities that they can adapt their own styles when necessary. For example, difficult and slow-to-warm-up children will often act irritable. If their parents provide calm support, affection, and clear direction, these young children usually develop a sense of security and learn to manage their anger.

No parent can respond with patience, structure, and warmth every time. If you are an active, take-charge type, for example, you may be continually baffled and frustrated by your anxious, slow-to-warm-up child. The conflict between your style and your child's temperament may become an ongoing battle. This is certainly not your fault or your child's, but simply a mismatch of styles. In two-parent families, the parent with the more compatible style may need to become more involved and more responsible for child-rearing in particularly difficult times.

> Seth was an active toddler, demanding and irritable with any new activity or change in his routine. His intense moods passed quickly, however, and he would move on quite cheerfully to something else.
>
> Seth's mother understood that his distractibility and impulsiveness could help her redirect his attention away from blowups and on to more appropriate play.
>
> Seth's father, however, had a hard time adjusting to his son's difficult temperament. Placid and easygoing, he was slow to anger and less intense than his wife or Seth. But once angered, he remained troubled and in a bad mood far longer. He could not distract himself and move on as quickly as Seth could. He found himself resenting his son because Seth did not seem to "care" when he misbehaved.
>
> Dad found it difficult to keep up with Seth's active pace and became less affectionate and less willing to play with him. Seth sensed his father's withdrawal and became more agitated and unsettled around him. He instinctively drew closer to his mother, who was also active, highly aroused, and excitable. Seeing their closeness, Dad felt more guilty, more withdrawn, and more resentful.

Guidelines to Assess If You Are "In Sync"

It is crucial to examine carefully the match between your own style and your child's. This will help you to identify more clearly how your child expresses anger and to track how you are helping or blocking him or her.

You can use the following suggestions to compare your own personality style to your child's, to see how closely you "match":

1. Begin by reviewing the parenting and problem-solving styles described in Chapters 4 and 5. Make sure you have a positive plan for you and your partner to balance your different styles.

2. Answer the questions in this chapter that follow the four basic temperaments. This time, however, answer *as if the questions applied to you.* Is your temperament "Easy," "Difficult," "Active," or "Slow-to-Warm-Up"?

3. If your answers indicate that the match between you and your child is close, you may have an easier time sensing what your child needs and tying your own behavior to this goal.

4. If the match is very different, you will have more of a challenge ahead. Don't let yourself become resentful of or withdrawn from your child; these are understandable feelings but will only create more problems. Do use the new tools you'll learn in this book to understand and to react positively to your child.

Can Stepparents, Adoptive Parents, and Foster Parents Be "In Sync"?

If you are a stepparent, an adoptive parent, or a foster parent, you face a special challenge. Your rhythms and temperament are much more likely to be a mismatch with a child who does not share your biological heritage. Irritations, tensions, and conflicts will arise from your physical differences, making it harder at times to establish a sense of bonding, security, and trust.

Emotional closeness may take longer to achieve and may delay the child's feelings of self-confidence and self-esteem. Both parent and child may need more emotional distance, yet somehow feel guilty and ashamed. The balance of privacy and intimacy may be more difficult to achieve. But hang in there! Your progress may seem slow and the ups and downs frustrating, but the skills in this book can work for you.

In the next chapter, you will find ideas to help you and your preschooler cope with the rages that often accompany young children's development.

9

Preschool Children

RAGES IN STAGES

Beyond the peaceful moments of teddy bears and lullabies, childhood is a time of changes and tension. Young minds and developing bodies are struggling to grow. Children move through predictable stages that involve mastering complex physical, emotional, mental, and moral changes. Learning to walk, for example, creates a sense of excitement and power, but it also brings anxiety and doubt.

How does a child balance the thrill of the first steps away from Mommy or Daddy with the fear of falling? How does a child balance the excitement of learning a new skill with the frustration that comes when Mom or Dad says, "Not right now"?

Developmental Tasks of Preschoolers

Each stage of growth and development is a balancing act, with unavoidable stresses and frustrations. You have a crucial role in teaching your child how to manage these inevitable conflicts. The struggle to achieve balance is the force that drives the Dragon of Anger as your young child strives to accomplish the following tasks between two and five years of age.

Physical Control: "It's My Body, and I'll Cry If I Want To!"

Children must learn control of their bodies. Children who develop good physical mastery of themselves have an easier time with the later stages of emotional development. When adults help children to soothe themselves and master their bodies, children can feel in control when they handle pain, hurt, and frustration. They can trust themselves when they have learned that they can count on adults to help.

Physical triggers in young children include pain, hunger, thirst, discomfort, and sudden changes in routine. If they cannot find comfort, they will feel frustrated and angry and may express those feelings through kicking, crying, screaming, or flailing their arms and legs. This intense physical activity is an attempt to find a release for physical tension.

Mastery: "I Can Do It Myself!"

In two- to five-year-old children, the desire to "do it all by myself"—to master self-control and language—peaks. Children are ready for so many new and exciting things. But watch out! When they are frustrated in their attempts to be in complete control, the result can be a raging storm of actions and words. Parents can easily be overwhelmed by these outbursts.

Preschoolers believe that parents know all and can cure all, yet they often resist our efforts to help them. They may reject the routines for soothing and satisfying that worked so well when they were toddlers; they no longer want us to take control. Children want to be master—but only until frustration sets in. Then they expect Mom or Dad to read their minds and soothe and satisfy them. But if you take over, you risk further frustrating your child's drive for independence and mastery.

Learning to Trust: "Do You Love Me?"

When parents can help a child soothe herself and master her body, she develops a sense of trust—trust that happiness is possible, that others care, that she can be secure, that one day she can be in control.

We all know that children need love. To be secure in our love, our children need us to help them master their bodies, and they must learn to trust that we will soothe them when anger, hurt, and frustration overwhelm them.

Emotional security in young children is the foundation upon which older children build positive self-esteem. Confidence in who they are allows them to have a better connection with others, a greater capacity for closeness, and a sense of empathy. The ability to understand themselves readies them for true caring and genuine intimacy. Without a sense of emotional security, children may feel profound self-doubts and lone-liness, which may fuel the Dragon of Anger.

Typical Anger Triggers in Preschoolers

The following triggers can make any of us angry! They are especially upsetting to young children.

- Frustration that they can't do it or have it all *now*
- Inability to coordinate a new skill
- Difficulty in expressing their needs
- Hurt
- Pain
- Disappointment
- Wanting something desperately, but being too tired or too little to do it
- Parents misunderstanding and failing to satisfy them
- Parents taking over, instead of asking how they can help

Temper Tantrums: Do They Have to Be?

Older children have the language to communicate their needs. Pre-schoolers haven't yet learned that words really can lead to satisfaction. For little children, words are demands, not tools for negotiation. If words don't yield immediate results, then a tantrum certainly will!

Temper tantrums are universal in children. Of course, they often occur at the worst times and places for parents. From embarrassment, we may find ourselves giving in at the grocery store or mall, offering whatever it takes to get our screaming child to stop crying. When we give in this way, we can feel humiliated to have been outmaneuvered by a powerful preschooler. Her anger has been effective in achieving desired results. She has won the candy in the checkout line.

Children whose tantrums are tolerated and reinforced are most at risk for emotional problems as adults. When children learn that whining, crying, and sulking are powerful ways to get others to do what they want *right now,* they become self-centered and narcissistic adults. Parents who give in and then respond with guilt, lectures, or ridicule do not correct the problem. They simply help to create adults who not only throw tan-trums but also become obsessed with guilt and self-recrimination.

Often, fatigue, illness, overstimulation, or other pressures trigger a tantrum. Doesn't your child need your support, love, and concern even more during these times? Certainly, but she does not need you to be controlled and manipulated by her rage. Your child needs you to show how calm can be restored and her needs met by using quiet words. You can teach your child more appropriate ways to *calm down* and *to use her words* to express her needs when she feels angry.

Success in achieving control of their bodies and emotions at this age helps children let go of tantrums, just as they have let go of their bottle and their teddy. If your child has not yet let go of tantrums, see Chapter 16.

Next, in Chapter 10, we will discuss the developmental challenges of school-age children and some techniques to teach them about resolving conflicts.

10

School-Age Children

THE IMPORTANCE OF BELONGING

Belonging, status, and achievement: These are the goals school-age children are trying to reach. If children feel different in any way, they will have a hard time developing a sense of belonging. For unathletic, unattractive, shy, anxious, or very active children, fitting in can seem impossible. If they are self-conscious about their looks and their abilities, insecure children may worry constantly that others will discover their worst weakness.

This stage can be particularly painful. School-age children do not yet understand that *we are all different* (not necessarily deficient) in some way. They have a remarkable ability to go for the jugular with teasing and put-downs that can expose the most painful wounds. How can they feel good about themselves, if others see them as weird, strange, or different?

The following sections provide some advice on how school-age boys and girls can learn the tools to handle conflicts peacefully.

How to Resolve Conflicts Peacefully

School-age children tend to overreact to criticisms and teasing from their peers. Try as we might, parents seldom succeed in helping our children to see put-downs and critical comments as jokes. Few children can "just ignore it." Many kids mistakenly believe that the only way to gain a sense of belonging and status with the group is to "win" every conflict, by physical force if necessary. It is a rare child who has the verbal and mental skills, and the moral reasoning ability, to solve problems without aggression.

Teach Your Child "No, Go, and Tell"

Elementary school children need rules to help them master the emotional, intellectual, and moral aspects of anger control. Following rules gives them a sense of mastery. Clear, simple rules can help establish a climate in which it is considered babyish and uncool to be a bully or to resort to fights to get your way. A climate that encourages self-control can help kids win battles against the angry Dragon.

Effective rules for school-age children begin with *No, Go,* and *Tell.*

• *NO: Teach your child to say "No" to acts of provocation, violence, and ridicule.* Help your child know he has the right to say, simply and positively, "I don't like that," and to offer other things to do or to play.

• *GO: If the "No" rule helps short-circuit the conflict, great. If not, teach your child to Go. Go do something else.* Walk away. Leave. Your child can make clear with his body that he is not going to participate in the dispute. Teach him to say nothing else. Then go do something fun; join another child in an activity.

• *TELL: If other children pursue him or another child persists in the argument, then your child must Tell.* Telling is not tattling. Telling is going for help. Let your child know she can go to an adult and tell what she has done to say "No" and to try to leave the battle. She can ask for help to divert the conflict and start something better to do. She can ask for help to mediate and solve the problem. Chapter 23 will give you more tools to help peers resolve conflicts.

Help Your Child Join the Group

When children have a way to belong, they may no longer feel so sensitive to teasing from other kids. Here are some things you can do to help your child be a part of the group while maintaining a needed sense of space:

1. *Encourage your child to watch how other kids handle put-downs.* They could make a joke, perhaps, or pretend not to hear, or go off to do something else. See Chapter 23 for more ideas.

2. *Help your child identify a special interest or ability.* If your child does not already have a major interest or hobby, give him or her opportunities to sample the possibilities in a low-key way. Surprise your child with a pile of paperback books, stacked on the nightstand. Get tickets for a baseball game or science exhibit. Spend Sunday afternoons cooking together. (Remember that your child's interests will probably be different from your own, which is great. Let your child teach you!)

3. *Meet with your child's teacher for help in understanding your child's role among classmates.* Ask for suggestions from the teacher and

find ways to help your child develop skills at home that will make it easier to fit in at school.

   4. *Encourage your child to find his or her own way to* belong, *not just to survive.*

   5. *Praise your child for finding ways to use brainpower—not fists— to feel in control.*

Issues That Affect School-Age Children

Insecurity

It is vital to help insecure children find some way to belong and fit in. They need to find some avenue of success, some way to achieve a sense of status that does not require a great deal of closeness. Following is an example of how parents can help.

> *Alan, a fourth-grader, was often on the sidelines at school because of his natural tendency to wait and watch. Classmates often became impatient with his cautiousness and reluctance, and rarely included him in group play. This only made Alan more anxious and more hesitant to join in. Even worse, he was branded as a "scrub" in athletic games and a "chicken" when any new activity came up.*
>
> *The other children soon decided that teasing Alan was fun. After years of being so shy and quiet, he was becoming a raging Dragon. It took a lot of teasing to set him off, but, of course, the gang of kids always managed. They loved to see Alan explode and make a fool of himself. A vicious cycle had developed. The teasing confirmed Alan's worst fears: He was indeed different and worthless, and he could never belong. As his loneliness and anger grew, he felt like running away to where no one would ever make fun of him again. Alone in his treehouse, he was obsessed with vivid fantasies of revenge.*

At first, Alan's parents disagreed about how to help him. His father was worried that Alan was fast on his way to becoming a wimp and had long argued that Alan should learn to stand up for himself. Alan's mother was more worried and cautious. She knew that all their previous attempts to push their son had led to even more withdrawals and sullen strikes.

Alan's parents met with his teacher, who gave them helpful information about Alan's problems at school. All agreed that Alan's interest in photography could be the key to greater self-confidence for him. Alan could create wonderful media images of his classmates. He could use an imaginary movie in his head to blast away his enemies, without having to do it in person. He could film videos of the school soccer team in action. He could take a leadership role in the class play without having to be center stage. Alan then had positive ways to belong. Since he no longer felt threatened by the teasing, he could stay cool. A wry sense of humor gave him effective comebacks to keep the teasing from bothering him.

Jealousy: "It's Not Fair!"

School-age children often seem obsessed with fairness. As you will see in Chapter 12, rules are important at this stage to provide a moral compass. Rules also provide a standard for group belonging and connection. Most kids complain, "It's not fair" when they feel left out, violated, or unloved. No matter how equal, consistent, and fair parents try to be, there are always the battles over who got the most.

As a wise parent, you can help your child see that life is not always fair or equal. You can try to understand why your child feels left out or unfulfilled. Fairness is an especially difficult issue with siblings; Chapter 24 will give you the tools and the confidence to do what is right for each child.

Blended Families: Enough Love to Go Around

Not only are school-age children trying to find a sense of belonging with friends; they also desperately need to find a sense of belonging and connection at home. They worry, *How do I fit in when I am growing and changing so fast? How do I belong when my family may be changing so fast?*

In blended families, the challenge to belong can seem insurmountable. Kids often view parents as preoccupied: doting on a new partner with (yuck!) affection, or courting the stepkids to win favor. Rearrangement of the home to accommodate new family members brings ample opportunity for conflict and jealousy about who gets what.

> *Twelve-year-old Missy was constantly crying, "It's not fair!" The oldest girl, she had become Mom's helper and confidante after her parents divorced. Although embarrassed to admit at school that she was from a divorced family, for fear of being seen as different, she seemed to be making the adjustment well at home. When Mom fell in love, Missy kept her distance from her soon-to-be stepdad. He was patient and understood that Missy needed to get close at her own pace.*
>
> *The fireworks started when Missy's stepdad and his kids moved in. Missy lost much of her space and her privacy. Although she had previously enjoyed her role as big sister, she now resented the little ones. She became a bossy tyrant, ordering others and raging when*

*she could not be Queen of the Mountain. She jealously complained
when others got something from her mom or stepdad. She rejected
her parents' attempts to talk to her and to spend time with her.*

*After a while, everyone stopped trying. Missy was so irritable that
no one wanted to be with her. Although they would miss her, they
were almost relieved when she threatened to leave and go to live
with her "real dad."*

Total equality and fairness is not a realistic solution for older children struggling to adjust to a blended family. Their interests and needs
for independence are changing. They may no longer be comfortable
playing with the younger children. Preteens need more space and privacy, but when they get it, they may feel left out.

Missy no longer had a comfortable place to fit within the family.
Mom had a new confidant and helper. There was enough love to go
around, but how could her mom and stepdad help Missy see? She was
making herself so hard to love.

Missy needed time apart and to be proud that she was mature
enough to do some things without the family. She also needed "together
time," especially with Mom, much more than any of the other children
did.

As Missy learned to trust that her stepdad would support these
changes, she decided he wasn't so bad after all. He accepted when she
invited him to coach her on an important school project. Although she
did not yet want to think of herself as his daughter, at least they had
found a small piece of common ground. Missy was finding new ways to
fit into her changing family.

Kids need time to recover from divorce and the doubts about "Will
my parents stop loving *me*, too?" They may find it very hard to believe
that there is enough love to go around. It's no wonder so many second
marriages are stressful. How do parents meet everyone's needs?

Here are suggestions to help school-age and preteen children fit in
to a new family:

1. Spend time alone with your child, doing some of the things you
   used to do.
2. Arrange for your partner to take over household responsibilities
   and care for the other kids so that you and your child can be
   together.
3. Give your child more responsibilities, appropriate for the oldest,
   in recognition of his or her status in the new family.
4. Sit down as a family to agree on new rules for privacy and
   respecting others' privacy.

5. Do not allow your child to enforce the rules. Make it clear that you and your partner will decide on and provide necessary discipline.

Anger as a Mask for Loneliness

In children, anger often masks profound hurt, loss, and low self-esteem. School-age children who are lonely and depressed often display aggressive behavior. For example, children who are adjusting to stress or loss may have unresolved feelings of depression and abandonment. These can lead to problems in school, at home, and with friends: An active or difficult child may show a lack of cooperation, refusal to obey rules, and fighting. A sensitive child may brood and fume.

Classmates tend to avoid aggressive children, which gives them even fewer chances to develop positive feelings about themselves. Many feel empty and inadequate. They may mask their vulnerability by appearing tough and strong.

Jessica's parents entered a substance abuse program when she was five. Her parents were consumed with their own recovery and focused most of their energies on managing the tremendous responsibilities involved in stabilizing themselves and dealing with their own emotions. Jessica had been a cheerful and accommodating child and was acutely sensitive to her parents' emotional needs. The little girl often "mothered" them and her younger brother. She tried to be perfect and hid her own needs.

Much later, the calls from her school began. Her teachers were concerned that Jessica could not sit still and follow the classroom routine. She was demanding, bossy, and aggressive with the other children, and no one wanted to choose her for a playmate. When her parents came to school for conferences, Jessica felt even more pressured, because she was afraid the meetings would make her parents argue about her. She lied to cover up problems, so as not to put more pressure on her parents.

By second grade, Jessica was even more explosive and uncontrollable. Her parents were called frequently to take her home. Her father reacted with frustration. He believed the school and Jessica's mother were too lenient, and he pushed them to be more firm and to discipline Jessica more often. The school and the mother believed that Jessica would defy any discipline. Jessica's mother was consumed with guilt and blamed herself for being too unavailable and too harsh.

Finally, Jessica was center stage. She was gaining the much-needed attention she had lost and craved. Unfortunately, this negative attention was costing her a considerable loss of status at school and creating tension between her parents. A school psychologist provided the consultation the family needed.

Each parent agreed to spend more time with Jessica, to counter her intense loneliness. Her father became a coach for her softball team. Together, father and daughter learned to emphasize cooperative team efforts. Her mother devoted more time to just "hanging out" with Jessica. As problems from her school and Mom's work came up, they helped each other find cooperative solutions and positive ways to reduce stress.

Your child may be using aggression to hide feelings of loneliness, but with help from you and your child's teacher, your child can learn nonaggressive ways to deal with frustration and loss. Here are some ideas to help you begin:

1. If you are a two-parent family, both parents need to agree to cooperate with the new plan.
2. Each of you must place high priority on spending time with your child.
3. Meet with your child's teacher to develop a consistent discipline plan, at home and at school. Your plan should:
   - set clear boundaries on aggressive behavior,
   - agree upon fines for misbehavior, and
   - develop rewards for times when your child plays cooperatively and settles conflicts without aggression.
4. Find healthy ways for your child to gain acceptance with peers. Invite classmates over. Join a club. Keep trying until your child finds a niche.

Embarrassed by Divorce

Although many children come from divorced homes, some children may never discuss their family situation. They are afraid of being embarrassed or losing status with their friends.

Eleven-year-old Tony's grades had slipped in the year after the divorce. Before they split up, his parents had helped him every night with his assignments, but that routine had been disrupted, along with so many other things in his life. Tony would daydream his way through class, which annoyed his teachers. Kids had started making fun of him for being so out of it.

Generally Tony was anxious and compulsive about following school rules; he didn't want to cause more trouble for his parents. On the playground, he needed to run and jump to release his tensions and extra energy. During the less-structured times in the school day, Tony became more out of control. Kids started calling him "Space Man" because of his oddball behavior. When teams were chosen for sports or projects, he was often the last one picked. His classmates sensed his vulnerability and teased him harder. He was an easy target; it was fun to see him blow up. Finally Tony exploded and broke a friend's nose. His parents were called in for a conference with the principal.

Tony's parents agreed that Tony's anger was masking deep depression and self-doubts. They allowed Tony to enter a school-sponsored group for children with divorced parents.

The group, led by the school psychologist, established rules for problem solving and expressing feelings. The children shared ideas and experiences and learned to show respect for and acceptance of each other. As Tony attended sessions with other kids from his school, he realized he was not alone and began to feel a sense of belonging.

Tony gradually became confident enough to use many of these skills with his classmates, but he still felt anxious about talking to his parents about his conflicts with them. The group leader prepared his parents and taught them how to listen to Tony's frustration, understand his anger, and change their routines so that Tony had more support and direction. Tony learned to stand up for himself without worrying that his parents would battle. He began to trust that they could work cooperatively in his behalf.

Many parents, still in conflict and wounded from a divorce, have difficulty agreeing on a plan of action to help their child. The best way for them to help may be to *ask for help*.

———————————

Belonging. Understanding. Trust. Build this security base at home. Help your school-age child develop a positive way to achieve status and to belong with friends. With this foundation, your child will be ready to learn the tools of peacemaking. Then you will both be ready for the inevitable storms of adolescence.

11

Adolescent Children

EXPECT REBELLION

Adolescents have a powerful need to belong and to fit in. They want to be in control of their bodies, but when puberty begins, hormones rage. Even easy children may become moody. Minor frustrations become land mines for angry battles. Power struggles with authority figures escalate. No matter how fair parents try to be and how reasonable teachers are, rebellion is the hallmark of this stage.

Many young teenagers feel very much out of control of their bodies at this stage; the physical changes seem both grotesque and exciting. Because they feel so overwhelmed on the inside, some teens may go to exaggerated lengths—exuding a very tough image, using brash sexual talk—to seem in control.

Peer Pressure

Group pressure can lead active teens to flagrant acts of angry behavior. Difficult teens may become anxious and prone to simmering rages. Slow-to-warm-up teens may become paralyzed in public and make mountains out of molehills at home. If challenged by adults, they are likely to rebel or to fly into a familiar and explosive rage.

Anxiety about puberty and dating can trigger teenagers' worries about whether they are lovable. This anxiety provides the fuel for many conflicts. Teens can work themselves and their families into explosive rages when they fear they won't be allowed to do something that "all my friends are doing." Battles about who makes the rules are often false fronts for deeper worries about whether the teen will be allowed to fit in with the group's plans, dress codes, and attitudes.

Anxiety about sexual attractiveness often drives teens to turn petty misunderstandings and unintentional slights into major wars. Peer conflicts build. Friends one day seem enemies the next. Slow-to-warm-up and easy teens may simply withdraw from these wars or resort to subtle tactics to retaliate and get revenge. Active teens may turn an unintended slight into a battle.

Teens Who Turn Violent

Teens with difficult and active personalities may be in for real trouble at this stage. An active teen, even with a relatively high self-esteem and a stable home base, may have problems with fighting and aggression. For active teens who have no support system and who live in high-conflict families or violent neighborhoods, serious trouble may lie ahead.

> Ty's mother complained that she could never keep up with him. She was often so preoccupied and depressed with her own stresses and job responsibilities that she had little time to focus on him, much less to keep track of where he went after school and at night. Her rules and limits were inconsistent. She was proud of her son's basketball talent, but then Ty was furious when he was taken off the team for poor grades. It seemed there was nothing his mother could do to stop the teachers' complaints about Ty's bad attitude.

Ty was finally getting some status. He was succeeding (however negative that success) as a tough guy. He could belong by overpowering. If anyone ridiculed, provoked, or crossed him, he was ready to attack and retaliate—particularly if someone upset his girlfriend. His schoolmates became the audience for his personal melodrama of "might makes right."

> One day, fighting for the honor of his lady, Ty cursed and shoved a teacher. As the principal tried to sort out the chain of events and decide what to do, she discovered that the teacher had given Ty's girlfriend a D—unaware that the low grade would result in the girl's being grounded and unable to go out with Ty that night. The worst of the tragedy was that Ty had bragged to many students that he wanted to kill the teacher. The crowd's rumor-mill fed the frenzy to violence.

Ty had achieved "status" through physical force. The tragedy was Ty's inability to master the real tasks of adolescence: learning to control his physical impulses and to belong to the group through emotional connection and closeness.

Peers become an effective motivator for change in teens like Ty. If Ty were not getting an audience for his violent actions, he could look at other choices. How different this incident would turn out, if Ty and his girlfriend received status for keeping cool, being good sports, and making good grades.

As adults we bear responsibility for our teens' values. We create the media messages that reinforce "might makes right." We tolerate violence in our schools and communities by not providing positive options. Teens need status and recognition for being peacemakers, for helping others. Appendix B will give ideas about how to promote peace in your school and community. Chapter 27 will give you advice on how to help a chronically aggressive teen.

Teens Who Fear Intimacy

Teenagers in some families may be caught in constant tension and disarray. The parent who avoids emotional issues fosters a climate of secretiveness at home. The teens may learn to mask their own needs and feelings to take care of the parent. They feel confused, powerless, and afraid. As these children grow, so does the anger inside.

But how should they express it? By avoiding any show of feelings and escaping to a fantasy world within their own imaginations? By joining their friends in drugs, shoplifting, or petty vandalism, to find a sense of belonging outside the family? Or should these teens express their frustration and rage through violence, to gain a sense of power and control that they never have at home?

> *Fifteen-year-old Josh's mother was an alcoholic. His father was an irritable man who had little sense of dignity and control in his work. He would come home in a foul mood, begin criticizing his children and demanding that his wife keep the kids at bay so that he could crawl into his shell.*
>
> *Josh's parents rarely argued violently; his mother tended to escape into her bottle, and his father retreated to the TV. At times, though, long-buried resentments erupted into raging arguments, followed by dramatic apologies, promises of better times, and an affectionate period of courting between his parents. Love and hatred, anger and aggression, caring and control—these powerful emotions became intertwined for Josh.*
>
> *As a teen, Josh swore he would never repeat his parents' mistakes. He refused to drink or take drugs. He managed to avoid the gangs and their lures into delinquent behavior. However, when he*

fell in love, his family legacy began to haunt him. If he felt hurt, anxious, abandoned, frustrated, or criticized, Josh only knew he was angry. He had never learned to tell the difference between other painful feelings and the anger his parents expressed.

As conflicts developed with girlfriends, Josh knew no way to respond except to imitate what he had learned at home—avoid the problem until his hidden rage exploded. Could Josh find a way to avoid the destructive patterns in his own family and learn to trust and feel close to other people?

A future of loneliness awaits teens who cannot control themselves physically and emotionally. True intimacy will be difficult for them. Their anger can build to aggression or turn inward, toward violence.

Fortunately, most teenagers *can* achieve a sense of inner balance and control. They can learn to reject violence and move toward trust and intimacy. If your teen is at risk, there are steps you can take to help immediately:

1. Make sure your teen has at least one adult who cares, who connects with him or her, and who can make a difference.
2. Give your teen a chance to belong in a peer group that has a sense of fairness and values.
3. Provide your teen opportunities to meet adults and other teens who have reached emotional and moral maturity.

This sense of control can make all the difference between a teen who feels chronically angry and disconnected, and one who can master anger and achieve a sense of intimacy.

Freedom for Teens

Most of us remember only too well those feelings of physical inadequacy that triggered our own teenage feelings of frustration and rage. We remember the powerful urge to be independent, to be grown up and on our own—and the firm conviction that our parents could never possibly understand how it felt to be caught in the never-land between childhood and adulthood.

Many of us will eagerly lend a sympathetic and advisory ear to a teen who feels ready to talk. It is far more difficult to weather the attacks and rages our teenagers aim directly at us. *We* are the most frequent targets of their rampages; *we* are often the enemy that keeps them dependent. We may have difficulty giving needed independence while accepting a teen's cry to "Trust me!" if what we see at home is one angry explosion after another.

Dependence versus Independence

Didn't we settle this issue back when our little ones moved out of diapers and into school? But during the teen years, the struggle peaks again. The teen's need for self-control often becomes so exaggerated that everything—emotions, thoughts, and morals—tilts out of balance. Nothing else seems to matter except the all-powerful need for independence.

> *Fifteen-year-old Tess had always been strong-willed but, through her early years, her parents had found good outlets for her to take charge. They had expected her adolescence to be stormy, but they were not prepared for how intensely Tess rejected them. She refused to come to meals and spent every minute either in her room or out with friends. Her parents could find no common ground; even going out to dinner and a movie (which she previously had enjoyed) was miserable. Tess either refused to talk or defensively exploded when her parents tried to make conversation.*
>
> *At first her parents thought this phase would pass. But her grades began to fall, and she was choosing a whole new circle of friends. Her parents worried that she might be drinking or sexually active. Tess exploded when her parents asked her to do housework or to tell them about where she was going at night. She begged her parents just to "trust" her. But how could they? She refused to give them any information about her plans, and her new friends just honked at the curb for her to come out.*
>
> *Her parents worried that Tess was dangerously out of control, and they wanted to clamp down with more restrictions. Even more, they worried that they might never even be friends with their soon-to-be adult daughter.*

Many parents have come to realize the hard way that the more they clamp down, the more their teens will rebel. It is crucial, however, to give teenagers a "safety net," a set of house rules that provide clear limits and consequences and help ensure safety and responsibility.

In the preceding example, with Tess as an equal (though reluctant and resentful) participant, she and her parents negotiated a list of ground rules. Tess could earn increasing freedom and have more "trust" only if she followed the rules.

Helping Your Teen Earn Freedom

You can help your own teen earn freedom without dropping out of the family. Here are some ideas to help you get started:

1. *Sit down with your teen and draw up a list of house rules, including curfews for school nights and weekends.* You might agree, for example,

that your teen can have free time with friends only if homework is done, grades stay up, and the curfew is respected. In Chapter 20, you will learn more about negotiating with a teen.

2. *Establish consequences for violations of the house rules.* Violations might result in more chores; when your teen has completed the extra work, freedom returns.

3. *Insist that your teen find some common ground with you.* Yes, your teen will probably resist this as "boring," but agree to spend time together each week as a family. Because many teens are eager to get their own job and car, you might ease into your new "family time" by spending a few Saturdays investigating resources for both of these goals.

4. *Agree not to nag and pry into each detail of your teen's life.* Trust must work both ways.

5. *Remember that your teen's struggles and conflicts are inevitable and normal.* Beware of further upsetting the balance either by coming on too strong or by helplessly giving up. Be a counterbalance.

6. *Help your teen find positive ways to control his or her body and temper.* Chapters 17 and 18 will give you some effective tools.

7. *Let go of your own need for absolute control.*

Humor, empathy, a listening ear, and a willingness to make the transition from boss to adviser will help all of you weather this difficult, stormy period. Soon (but never soon enough) your teen will regain a sense of physical control, and the tirades will become less intense. Your teen will find areas of independence and develop some common ground of closeness.

With time and patience, you can help your teenager accept that parents can be allies, provided that your teen makes good on the promise to "trust me." Believe that after your teen achieves much-needed independence, you will once again be friends.

12

Teaching
Morality

CAN THE FIERY DRAGON
BE CIVILIZED?

If you have tried to correct problems in your own anger style, if you have provided an honest, caring model of how to correct mistakes, if you have continued to care and to reach out through your child's tirades, you have done your best.

Still, many parents and teachers worry, *Can our children truly learn to be good and kind, when there seems to be so much violence and hatred in the world? What can I expect from a child who has watched thousands of hours of violent cartoons and killed untold "enemies" on the video screen? What does the future hold for children who, often at a very young age, have been exposed to violence not only on TV and in the movies but also in their own communities and families? We can try to provide positive examples, but how can we trust that today's children will find a moral compass?*

These questions, age-old and debated through changing generations, still have no easy answers. This chapter will not presume to tell you what specifics to teach your children about morality and ethics. You can find guidance in those areas within your own family's beliefs, from your own experience, and from the moral teachings of religious and philosophical leaders. Instead, this chapter's discussion, which is solidly based on psychological research, focuses on the process of moral development in children. You will learn how the stages of moral development relate to children's ability to manage and express their anger constructively.

The Stages of Moral Development

Just as children develop physically, intellectually, and emotionally in stages, they also have changing and evolving moral capacities. The following moral stages are universal.

- Early childhood, during which children are self-centered beings, who use tantrums and physical force to get what they want for immediate gratification
- School age, during which children learn to use rules and social norms to gain approval for making caring and responsible choices
- The teen years, during which young people develop the flexibility to balance their own rights in a respectful and caring way with the rights of others

Teaching Morality by Example

"Spare the rod and spoil the child" has long been a tenet of moral teaching. Ruling with an iron hand, however, and making your home a dictatorship is not the answer. Of course, discipline is important. At all stages, children need and want rules to live by. Positive discipline can be an effective teacher, as you will read in later chapters. As you discipline, try to be calm and in control of your angry emotions; supportive and not critical; flexible and not rigid.

Whatever your child's age or stage, your modeling and example are the best strategies to teach morality—and are far more effective than lectures. (Children are masters at tuning out lectures.) Your child will learn by observing the adults in his or her world; your example is a powerful guide.

Small children are intellectually incapable of thinking about what they are doing and why. Of course, they may ask "Why?" many, many times, but they cannot truly understand cause and effect. It is futile to ask preschoolers, or even most school-age children, *why* they are angry. Usually the "why" question just makes you more frustrated and your child more confused—and more angry.

Your goal is to help your child develop his or her physical, emotional, intellectual, and moral capacities to control the Dragon of Anger. You can begin by teaching your child through your example how to stop using words as weapons and to start using words as tools for resolution and healing. You also can help an older child learn to balance what he or she wants with what someone else wants, and then to compromise.

Your child will learn to think by working through your family's rules, examples, and experiences. Clear thinking can be an effective rein on the Dragon of Anger. To be successful, the thinking must be simple. The goal is to teach a school-age child to tell himself, "Stop yelling. Start thinking about what I can do to calm down. Then I can work with Mom (or Dad, or my friends, or my teacher) to try to get what I want." An older child might learn to add, "Maybe *both* my friend and I (or my parents and I) can get a little of what we want."

Guidelines to Encourage Moral Development

You can set the stage for grown-up solutions by making rules about what your family can and cannot say during arguments and conflicts and deciding what methods you will use to settle problems, depending on your child's age and temperament. The following are suggestions for establishing guidelines during the predictable stages of your child's moral development.

Early Childhood: Learning That It Can't Always Be "Me First"

Children first begin to recognize their emotions during the preschool years. As their language skills develop, they look for a name for everything. It is important to remember, however, that even though your child may be able to *name* his feelings, he does not yet understand those feelings in relation to other people. A three-year-old believes that the sun and moon follow him and rise and fall for his benefit. Emotions are important, because they meet his needs, and his alone. His language about feelings is self-serving; if he can name it, he may gain some control over whatever is happening around him. Thinking errors about feelings begin here; some children (and adults) can remain frozen at this stage of self-centeredness throughout their lives.

As preschool children learn to interpret emotions, they focus first on how to get their own needs met. They see other adults and children as either helping or blocking them from getting what they want. Typical preschoolers' angry comments include, "You make me mad!" "I hate you!" "I want that!" "Gimme!" At about age five, children recognize that emotions and actions are related, but they still concentrate on their own self-centered needs: "If you don't give me that, I won't be your friend." "I hate you; I won't do it."

> Scotty was a big, strong boy for four years old. He could easily overpower and outmaneuver any child his age if both wanted the same

toy. His mother provided day care for many younger children, and Scotty often resented her taking care of "the babies." He could not, however, explain his complex feelings of jealousy or of his longing for his mother to care for him in the same way that she took care of the younger children. Instead, Scotty began to stage seemingly unprovoked tantrums more often and more stormily. He began to dominate the other children and to grab their toys away.

When his mother tried to set limits, Scotty ran out of the time-out corner or hit her back if she spanked him. He would yell, "I hate you! You're not my mom!" Scotty's mother knew she needed a more effective strategy, but what could she do to tame her out-of-control little boy?

Scotty was excited by the power and control he was gaining, but he was still not satisfied. He was not learning to control his body or his emotions. He could not communicate what he needed. He did not respect others' space, property, or needs, and the other children did not respect his.

What should his mother do to help him? Set increasingly firm limits and establish greater control? Or would this approach just create more resistance and more battles for control?

Help Your Bossy Child Learn Control. Young children need opportunities for self-control, status, and attention. Parents can show self-control by their own example, and then teach and encourage their children to use those ways.

Scotty's mother decided to make him her assistant. Scotty was to be in charge of helping the little ones to be patient and to share, to help them talk about their feelings and the feelings of others, and to help them calm themselves more independently. His mother would "pay" him by giving him extra privileges and extra time with favorite toys after the day care children had left.

The following steps show one way you can help your child gain new status while mastering emotional self-control and learning cooperative play.

1. *Assign your child a new job that offers a chance to be patient and to share with other children.* You can "pay" your child with an extra privilege or special time with you.

2. *Before the new job begins, give your child practice time with you.* Use puppets, dolls, or stuffed animals to make up a story about how to talk to a friend and play together. (This practice time will also give your child more time with you.)

3. *During the practice time, let your child take charge of setting the rules for fair play.* Your child will learn cooperative play skills and to use language to communicate feelings.

4. *Deflect your child's bossiness by insisting that the new job remain a secret from the other children.* Help your child understand that doing the job means showing the other kids, *by example,* how to be fair and how to share.

5. *Do not reward your child for bossiness.* You may want to deduct from your child's "earnings" (privileges or extra time with you) for bossy or aggressive behavior. You may also have your child practice the rules more often or give up any turns with favorite toys when other children were around.

Set Limits on Aggressive Behavior. The early years are children's most self-centered phase. They cannot yet understand cause and effect. They do not realize that their rages, selfishness, and tantrums can cause hurt and pain in others. Gradually, their language skills allow them to label their own and others' feelings. However, true empathy, real perspective-taking, and even simple moral choices are still beyond their abilities.

Therefore, preschoolers, particularly, need limits and boundaries to help them gain control of their physical rages and to learn to think about and respond to the rights and needs of others. If the limits you set are aggressive and hurtful, this is the model of morality you are providing. Aggression is not the most effective way for small children to show their anger, and, studies indicate, it is not even their primary choice. Unfortunately, all too often aggression is the path they are taught to take by grown-ups' words and actions.

> *Matt was a "typical boy" who fit all the stereotypes: active, curious, physically strong. An active child from birth, he wanted to be in control. Strong-willed and feisty, he often dominated other children. When he did not get his way, he shouted and hit—and thus quickly trained his playmates to give him whatever he wanted.*
>
> *In school he would grab, dominate, and win. Even children who were usually cooperative and communicative would act bossy and aggressive when they played with Matt. They quickly figured out that the only way to deal with him was to give him a dose of his own methods—grabbing, shouting, and hitting. Matt seldom had a chance to see friends solving problems peacefully.*
>
> *At home, Matt's mother lectured and warned Matt about his temper, but she failed to follow through or set any limits on his outbursts. Matt's dad took pride in his "manly" son. He would respond to Matt's aggressive displays of anger only if they threatened his own authority. Dad's yelling, threatening, and spanking showed Matt that aggressive strategies worked; they controlled other people. Soon Matt had the upper hand.*

Although he was an active child, Matt may not have been instinctively aggressive. From early childhood, however, he had learned that his aggression was his most powerful (and most frequently reinforced) action for expressing his anger. With his strong will and physical ability, Matt could have become a leader without resorting to aggression. He could have become much more effective in his relationships with his playmates and his parents if he had learned to control his impulses, communicate his feelings, and practice compromise instead of domination.

Active children can be difficult to tame, but even they crave limits and boundaries. All children want to be accepted and to belong. Bartering, rewards, and simple, positive consequences are excellent strategies at this stage.

If angry children continue to get what they want by using aggression, they will never become moral and responsible. If, however, they clearly understand that aggression will not get them what they want, they will move toward more peaceful ways to express their anger.

Promote a Sense of Pride and Caring. Without limits, boundaries, and adult examples at this key stage, preschool children will not learn to be fair and caring when they are angry. Fear of punishment, disapproval, and failure will lead to shame. Shame can lead to guilt and humiliation. Humiliation can prevent children at this stage from developing an essential emotional security base. Shame also can fuel the rage of difficult and slow-to-warm-up children.

> *Chrissy, a difficult child, became easily frustrated by the demands of preschool. Getting dressed, remembering to use the bathroom, and making friends all seemed overwhelming. Tense and worried, Chrissy was so preoccupied with her own needs for control that she was seldom tuned in to other children's actions or words. She often preferred to play alone because she could quickly become overloaded, stressed, and explosive.*
>
> *Chrissy's parents were often called in for conferences to discuss her seemingly unprovoked tantrums and attacks on other children. It was tempting for her parents and the preschool teachers to use lectures and shaming, because Chrissy always looked so guilty and seemed so upset after an outburst, hysterically crying, "I'm sorry!" But her anxiety and tension level continued to build. Soon, her tirades had become so fierce and unpredictable that her teachers threatened to expel her from preschool.*

Anxious children spend enough time shaming and criticizing themselves. They certainly do not need this approach from concerned adults.

Difficult and anxious children need examples of how to be calm and in control and how to follow the rules to be liked by others. When her parents, teachers, or playmates praise her attempts to be calm and to make good choices about following the rules, Chrissy learns a sense of pride. Shame simply makes her feel worse. As others help her feel good about herself, she can start using her sensitivity to feel good about others.

The best discipline is positive rewards for positive actions. Difficult children will learn to take another person's perspective and to consider others' rights and feelings if they first gain a sense of self-control. Naturally sensitive, they can learn to share and cooperate with rules, if given simple strategies and positive feedback.

School-Age Children: Learning to Care about the Group

Belonging, status, acceptance. School-age children, ages six to twelve, are struggling to put away their self-centeredness and to mold themselves to the group. Rules are vital at this age. Succeeding at the rules gives a child the chance to gain the group's acceptance. Rules often force a child to think about the goals and motivations of the other person or the other team.

Conflicts typically arise at this stage over whose rules the child will follow. For example, you might be so proud of your child's first attempts at baseball or card games that you let her make her own rules. It can be funny at first when she always sets up the rules so that she can win. Later it can become exasperating when your child seems to want to win at any cost and throws full-blown temper tantrums when things don't go her way.

Learning to Follow the Rules. Fortunately, the drive to belong is stronger than the self-centered drive to win. Rules create a safe climate in which children learn to work for the good of the group or the team. Rules apply in situations where everyone needs a chance to succeed, a turn at being OK. They are especially important for difficult, active, and slow-to-warm-up children. For them, rules provide a structure for being in control of out-of-control bodies and feelings. Rules let children look outside of themselves and consider the good of all. The best rules are not decisive or punishing but create a sense of shared purpose.

Children will rebel in a variety of ways against dictatorial rules at this stage. An active child may hit and run; a difficult child may resort to deception or power struggles; a slow-to-warm-up child may just shut down and go on strike. All children may resort to lying.

> *Kyle, an active child, often had trouble following any rules—at home, at school, or with friends. He was so busy and impulsive that he would seldom stop to think about what was expected of him now, because he was already three steps ahead of everyone else. However,*

Kyle was eager to succeed at sports, and he had the physical talent to be an athlete.

His parents were embarrassed at the physical tantrums Kyle threw, not only at practice, but even during his team's baseball games. His coaches and parents tried punishments, lectured him about the need to follow the rules, made him sit out of games, and warned that no one would want to play with him if he didn't shape up.

Kyle's tantrums leveled off, but he started arguing incessantly about the rules and lying about whose fault it was when he struck out or failed to catch a ball. When no one accepted his version, he would explode in anger, then pout stormily on the bench. How could Kyle gain a sense of status, learn to follow the rules, and learn to pace himself with other children?

For active children, structured experience is the best teacher. Kyle needed to realize that others valued his skills, but not his angry outbursts. He needed to make some hard decisions about how he would accept group rules and adult limits when he was out of control. He needed some incentives for respecting his teammates' rights, so the balance could swing away from his own self-centered needs. He also needed to choose a sport where he could compete at his own pace and work for personal bests *and* team success.

Lying and Misbehaving. Most children who lie or misbehave are not evil or defiant, but simply misguided. Many school-age children mistakenly resort to lies and rule violations to regain a sense of status and belonging. Lying peaks during this stage and is a very normal part of development. However, in children who feel an intense need to belong, bragging and boasting can become habitual lies, because they seem like shortcuts to getting around the rules.

Children lie for two main reasons: to avoid getting in trouble, and to increase their status. Both reasons are linked to the child's feelings of shame and guilt at being wrong, less "good" than the group, or not OK. Harsh·criticism and rigid discipline can make him or her even more desperate for approval and can make the lying worse. Shaming and blaming can make a child, especially a slow-to-warm-up or a difficult child, feel so worthless that lies can seem like the only way to save face.

Ben's parents had come a long way. Vowing not to repeat the mistakes of their own parents, they had stayed away from spanking and tried hard not to be rigid and authoritarian. They believed that if they treated Ben with honesty and respect, he would become honest and respectful.

Ben was generally a "good boy," and he hated to get into trouble. With other kids, Ben always had to be right and always wanted to be the best. During the inevitable turf battles, Ben would protest that "He started it," and was quick to blame the other guy. His parents, who usually had not seen the conflict, tried hard to find out who really had started it. By asking questions, they hoped to find out which child's version was "the truth." Ben often seemed so convincing in his denials that his parents believed their son and punished the other child.

Over and over, his parents heard complaints that Ben had lied about problems to avoid punishment. Lectures about telling the truth, threats to lose privileges, extra fines for lying—nothing seemed to work. His parents realized that Ben simply could not admit that he had been out of line. He lacked the confidence, or the ability, to admit when he had made even the smallest mistake. A sensitive and worried child, he could not deal with his sense of shame.

Ben's parents stopped playing private investigator to get at the truth. They realized trying to find out who started the disagreement encouraged lies. They tried a new approach: Whenever conflicts occurred, they assumed that each child had played a role. They avoided words such as "fault" and "blame." They made it clear that there would be no tattling. Ben and the other kids could come to the parents only for help in solving the problem. Ben could say what he had done to solve the problem, how he had gotten stuck, and what mistakes he would like to correct. The parents would be resources to help find solutions that would be acceptable to each child. Each child would be responsible for making things right.

Now Ben no longer worried about who was going to be found wrong and punished. If each person was always a little wrong and a little right, he did not have to worry about being singled out as the bad guy. He did not need to lie so much, and his tattling greatly decreased. For the first time, he could admit he was wrong. More important, he could think ahead for what he could do to make things right again.

Considering the Needs of Others. All of us have an innate capacity to sense the distress and hurt of others, a survival mechanism that has been good for individuals and for society since civilization began. Even infants can tune in to the distress of a parent or another child. This ability is called *taking perspective* and is a key element in children who use anger in a positive way to solve problems. Through careful teaching, we can help refine our children's ability to take another's perspective.

Learning to recognize and consider other people's feelings and needs, as well as their own, begins in school-age children. Identifying with and being accepted by their peers is most important at this age. You can help your child learn to balance angry feelings with considering the thoughts, feelings, and rights of others. The following are three key ways to begin.

- Set clear, consistent rules for behavior.
- Try to create learning opportunities and experiences that allow everyone to be a little bit right and a little bit wrong.
- Present situations in which everyone is responsible for the solution. When mistakes occur, everyone can negotiate rules and focus on agreeable solutions.

"Thinking Errors" among School-Age Children. Thinking errors are rampant on the elementary school playground: "He started it!" "She made me mad!" "It's not my fault!" "It's not fair!" It is no accident that children often make these statements in response to conflicts at this age. They are learning to use their thoughts to interpret and choose responses to their anger. Of course, many of their interpretations remain self-centered or self-justifying. You can help your child by letting her know that, even though she may feel very angry and upset, she still has a choice about how to respond. You can remind her to consider the rights and feelings of others. Then you can prompt her and show, by example, the beginnings of mutual understanding and compromise.

> At eight, Kate was thrilled by her newfound mastery of her body: "I can do it all by myself! I can get what I want. If you can't get me what I want, you make me mad!" Thus, Kate reasoned, it's OK to use her full-blown repertoire of parental modification techniques: persuasion, guilt induction, whining, and, of course, the temper tantrum.

Kate's thinking error proceeded as: "I want my way; you make me mad, and I am fully justified in using whatever it takes to get what I want." Kate's parents can help her move through this stage of self-justified rage toward greater self-control and awareness of others. They must understand her needs, then make it clear to her that, even if she is angry, she cannot get her way by hurting others or staging a tantrum. They must give her choices about more appropriate ways to express what she wants.

Another common thinking error is "He made me do it." How often do we adults justify our own outrage and revenge fantasies by saying, "He deserved it for making me . . . "? (In children's terms, we're saying, "You started it.") Generally, both people in this type of conflict believe that the end justifies the means, a view that often leads to further aggression and more intense anger, no matter how sophisticated the means of expressing it.

Children are primitive in their thinking patterns. Because they still view themselves as the center of the universe, they believe that whatever they want or need should be an immediate priority. It is rather unfair to expect them to consider the needs and feelings of others, without adult prompting, when they are just developing the ability to think about their own feelings.

When your child comes home and tells you that her friend is now her hated enemy, or that a bully has hurt her, you may feel tempted to justify and reinforce her version of the event. You might sympathize over her friend's "betrayal" or encourage her to stand up for her rights and hit that bully back. Much harder, but more effective, is asking her to consider the other child's position.

It takes time to ask enough questions to find out "the other side"— the details your child does not immediately remember or does not want to talk about. It can be frustrating to help her think of ways that she and the other child can find a common ground for compromise. Your efforts, however, are worth the time and frustration, because you will be teaching your child constructive ways to express and resolve anger.

There will always be "reasons" for anger. How we respond to those dragons is a matter of personal choice, training, and experience. We must, however, teach our children that, no matter what the trigger, we are not justified in using vicious words or violent behavior to express our anger.

Morality in the Teen Years

During adolescence, children's developmental history catches up with them. If they did not master important physical, emotional, and intellectual tasks along the way, they will continue to struggle with them. Teens cannot master moral dilemmas until they have achieved physical and emotional self-control.

For young people who have never experienced soothing, love, acceptance, belonging, or status, anger may erupt and explode. Some may react violently to minor slights or criticisms. If teenagers do not trust other people and do not believe that anyone will listen or want to understand, they will not even try to see another person's viewpoint. These teens may seem forever stuck, trying to relearn the lessons of earlier stages.

For teens who have struggled with poor self-control, poor self-esteem, and rejection all of their lives, adolescence will be a difficult time. Rage is likely to erupt in those who have experienced abuse, loss, and trauma. Some teens may turn their anger inward to self-punishing acts. Depression, suicidal gestures, and threats can occur. Eating disorders, headaches, and anxiety attacks can paralyze a sensitive teen. Relationships can be stormy, filled with jealous rages, possessiveness, tirades, and rejections.

An angry teen might justify delinquent acts with immature thinking. Some may justify senseless gang violence and destruction because of a distorted need for control and belonging to the group, at any cost. Unfortunately, the gang provides a sense of connection so vital to teens and a clear sense of rules (however warped) so crucial to moral development. These teens need fun, active ways to belong and achieve status. Healthy outlets provide opportunities to learn the moral tasks they may have missed at earlier stages.

Anger Over What Is "Right."   Even for teens who have seemingly done very well at earlier developmental stages, angry outbursts over what is right and fair can seem never-ending. It is no easy task to balance our own needs and wants with those of others. It is never easy to maintain a sense of accomplishment and intimacy. Conflict, anger, and moral dilemmas are universal, lifelong struggles. Teens can become so overwhelmed by and caught up in a headlong clash of emotions that their judgment lacks balance.

> *Sixteen-year-old Karen was an outspoken crusader for environmental causes. Her particular target was the corporation that employed her parents and carried a long record of industrial pollution. Karen's parents, liberal in their style and open in talking about issues and feelings, had been proud of how little discipline their daughter had needed as a youngster and how responsible she had become. Now, however, they were concerned about how increasingly zealous Karen had become in her political activities.*
>
> *When Karen violated the law during a demonstration outside their company, her parents were embarrassed and even more worried. Karen had become so outrageous in her anger that she had become a favorite source for the local TV news crews, filmed for dramatic effect.*
>
> *Family time at home became one long argument. Karen's friends soon stopped calling her to try to plan activities, with the excuse that she was always so busy with her mission, but really because they resented her antagonistic zealousness. Her boyfriend broke up with her after she stood him up several times to attend environmentalists' rallies.*
>
> *Her parents' dilemma was especially difficult, because they believed that Karen's cause was just and that even her anger was legitimate. Yet, she was letting the cause consume her; she was losing the intimacy of friends and family. Her anger was too intense and too frequent. How could her parents help her?*

Karen's parents knew that trying to restrict her from her political cause would only make the problem worse. Increasingly, they felt guilty;

maybe *they* were the problem. Maybe they needed to assume more responsibility for correcting the environmental problems they had, in part, created. By recognizing this possibility, they created the opportunity for common ground and mutual respect with their daughter.

They set aside time to work with Karen to promote environmental change. Karen balked at first, resentfully calling her parents' efforts insincere and patronizing, but the shared activities eventually reestablished a sense of intimacy. Secretly, Karen was pleased that she had achieved her parents' recognition. As her self-esteem grew, she no longer felt the need to be so self-righteous.

Karen also did some thinking on her own. She considered the feedback from her friends, who told her that her angry cause had become selfish and preachy, no matter how legitimate and valid it had been. Karen faced several emotional confrontations with her friends, as well as continuing conflict with her parents, as her family struggled to create a new balance of intimacy and mutual respect.

As Karen began spending part of her considerable energy on relationships, her friendships blossomed again. Minor conflicts with her parents continued, but the wrenching arguments over position and status subsided. Karen was even hired as a summer employee at her parents' corporation, as a research assistant on consumer and environmental issues.

Develop a Moral Compass in Your Teen. Following are some guidelines to help your teen develop good judgment when making moral choices.

1. *Be a good role model.* Talk to your teen about the choices you make each day. How do you balance your needs with the rights of your family, friends, and coworkers?

2. *Let your teen advise you.* Moral choices are tough. Often there are no absolute rights or wrongs. Talk together about the choices you face. Emphasize the consequences of possible choices and how your decision will affect others.

3. *Be an adviser to your teen.* Absolute dictums will cause any teen to rebel or reject your advice. Generate choices and help your teen broaden his or her ideas. Discuss the implications of each choice. Then let your teen decide.

4. *Emphasize our connections with others.* In the decisions you and your teen make, always show consideration for the feelings, needs, and rights of others. If your teen can take another's perspective, she can make sound moral decisions.

———————————————

Anger erupts when children, whatever their temperament and style, are out of balance. Even when they have found a fragile balance between body, mind, and emotions, children grow older and must face the challenges of a new developmental stage. Of course, conflicts are unavoidable. In the next part of this book, you will learn how to help yourself and your child be in better control of the physical arousal that is such a frightening element of the Dragon of Anger.

PART III

OLD AND NEW DRAGON PATTERNS

13

Recognizing the Dragon's Old Patterns

You are sensitive enough to recognize that your own anger and your reactions to your child's outbursts may be part of the problem. It's time to take heart. You can make tne difference in Taming the Dragon of Anger and finding solutions to your child's anger and your own. The first step is to stop the buildup of rage.

Assessing Your Own Dragonlike Reactions

Anger is not an isolated emotion; one source of its power is that energy, positive and negative, usually comes with it. Channeled constructively, this energy can become a powerful motivator for change within a family.

In this chapter, you will learn how to change your family's anger patterns, before they reach the explosion point, by recognizing the patterns and using simple ways to stop the escalation. You then will be ready to use the energy from anger in more constructive ways: to communicate, to discipline, and to solve problems.

Marty was new at being a single parent and facing the demands of three-year-old Becky and ten-year-old Brad. The children's mother had recently moved to another city, to try to get her life together and solve her serious alcohol-abuse problem. Marty realized that he and the kids were under a lot of stress from all the changes in their lives, but he was not prepared for their newfound moodiness and explosive-

ness. Before their mother left, they had been such quiet, eager-to-
please children, who tended to hide their feelings.

All Marty wanted was to be able to pick them up at day care,
have a peaceful evening, and enjoy some play time. But the children's
constant bickering and whining were getting on his nerves. Exhausted from his hard days at work, Marty found himself doing all
the things that his parents had done to him and that he had sworn
he would never do:

- Barking orders: "Sit down and shut up, or you're going to bed
  without dinner."
- Making empty threats: "Do you want to lose TV time for a
  month?"
- Trying a guilt trip: "Don't you want our family to be a happy
  place?"
- Reasoning: Lecture #9286 on why the kids should be kind to each
  other.
- Giving in: Often, from exhaustion, he would give in, thinking,
  Just this once won't matter. Out of concern for how the kids
  might be feeling after a phone call from Mom, he would appease
  their stormy tirades.

Whatever he did just seemed to make the problem worse. Becky and
Brad whined more and threw their tantrums more often. Would they
ever become a happy, peaceful family?

Parents often become part of the anger pattern that fuels, rather
than soothes, their children's anger. They may feel immobilized and powerless and spend too much time dwelling on what they are doing wrong.
They may mistakenly believe they are bad parents. Overwhelmed, they
may have little energy to think about the positives.

Before your child can change, you will have to handle your own
feelings, which are an important part of the Angry Dragon's patterns in
your family. The following are suggestions to help you assess your Dragon
pattern and focus your energy on creating positive responses to conflict.

Listen to What You Say

Whatever your parenting style, you can learn to recognize and avoid the
common responses that are virtually guaranteed to raise the anger level in
your family. By tracking yourself for a few days, and really listening to what
you say, you will learn a great deal about your family's anger patterns. You
then will be ready to try the strategies discussed in later chapters.

Shortly after the divorce, Marty had failed to set any limits on Becky and Brad. He was too permissive because he knew that the children were hurting. He was worried about the damage the divorce had done and obsessed about how to make it better. He did not want to come down hard on them, as his own father had done to him.

As the children became more out of control, Marty switched to lectures and long discussions. He had liked having his own mother explain "why" to him, and he also felt guilty about the divorce. He wanted to compensate by talking things out. Now, however, when angry outbursts were happening daily, Marty thought it was time to lay down the law.

We hate it when our children use nasty words, yet many of us are also guilty of feeding the Dragon of Anger when we resort to put-downs, criticisms, name calling, complaining, blaming, threatening, or barking orders. We feel ashamed when these hurtful words come flying out in the heat of anger. We feel out of control because these responses make the problem so much worse.

Listen to How You Say It

You may not be aware of how your anger has built until you are caught in its intensity. Then you may feel that, because you are so angry, you have to do something, so you keep talking. Many parents believe that talking is always the best response, because it helps get people's feelings out in the open. However, when you are really angry and out of control, most talking just adds fuel and pushes the conflict toward explosion.

What tone of voice do you use when you're angry at your child? Does your volume go up as your child's does, or do you provide an example of calmness and quiet? We all hate it when our children yell, whine, sigh, groan, or snarl at us, but once the angry sounds start, they can be contagious. Your own nasty tone of voice can become a catalyst for more heated anger. Silence is one of your most effective tools in taming the Dragon.

Do You Use Threatening Gestures?

Remember, too, that your actions speak far louder than words. Raised fists, clenched teeth, an accusing finger—all of these signal that anger is about power and confrontation. When you tower over your child, you magnify the imbalance of power between you and fuel the power struggle. When you turn away from your child, you make him or her feel unimportant and more likely to do something more drastic to get you to listen.

Do You Spank Your Child?

Almost every parent has used a quick swat, particularly with toddlers who are in danger of hurting themselves. However, just because a swat is immediately effective does not mean it is appropriate in the long run. Spanking teaches children that aggression is OK.

Children must learn that aggression is NEVER an acceptable means of dealing with anger in the family. The subtleties of "It's OK for me to spank you, but not OK for you to hit your brother when you want his toy" are lost on children. Parents should learn to set effective limits on their children's aggressive behavior. More important, we must serve as examples to teach our children to handle feelings and conflicts without aggression. Our actions will show our children how to communicate feelings with respect and consideration for the rights and needs of others.

Recognizing your own anger patterns, as you have learned to do in this chapter, is an important step in Taming the Dragon. You can best teach your child by your example. In the next chapter, you will build on your new understanding by examining the five myths about anger that block many parents.

14

Five Myths about the Dragon

Understanding the Myths

Many parents have problems responding constructively to their children's anger because they believe certain myths about the Dragon of Anger. The most widespread—and most dangerous—myths follow.

Myth #1: *I must get my child to admit what he did wrong.*

Everyone involved needs to accept responsibility when a problem occurs. However, the time to do so is not in the heat of a blowup. Figuring out who started it, or whose fault it is, adds fuel to a rage. When we are angry and upset, we are not in the mood for accepting blame or apologizing. Give everyone time to calm down and cool off before trying to resolve the problem. Then focus on what can be done to make things right. Make a plan to keep the problem from recurring.

Myth #2: *I must get my child to explain* why *she's mad.* Or: *I must get my child to explain* why *she did what she did.*

It is futile to try to force your child to reason when she is angry and upset. A Queen of the Worried parent may believe she can't respond correctly until she knows why her child is mad. Questioning and probing quickly escalate to nagging and shaming, fueling the child's fiery rage. Quiet discussions about "why" are appropriate for *later*, after the argument has ended and all of you feel calm and ready for the communication skills discussed in Chapters 19 and 20.

Myth #3: *My child should respond to reasoning and moral guidance.*

Of course, you have an important role in teaching your child values and moral decisions. But timing is crucial. In the heat of battle, your child will not respond to lectures and reasoning. When you are angry, your reasoning often has more to do with supporting your position than considering the common good. Your child may rightfully feel that a moral lecture is just another parent power tactic to win the argument. Remember: True authority calls for brevity and leadership. Teach by example.

Myth #4: *My child is out of control, so I must punish now.*

This myth is particularly troublesome for parents whose style tends toward King of the Mountain. Certainly parents should discipline for rebellious defiance, refusal to follow family rules, and aggressive outbursts of anger. However, timing is important. If you act too quickly, because of your own anger, your discipline will seldom be fair, and your child will not see it as a learning tool. In the heat of anger, many parents tend to punish out of a desire for revenge and control. It is almost always better to wait until you have had time to cool off. Then you can think about fair consequences that you can enforce and from which your child can learn.

Myth #5: *If I set limits, my child will just act more defiant and out of control. Or: If I set limits, I may be stifling feelings that need to come out.*

Parents whose styles tend toward the Appeaser or Queen of the Worried have particular difficulty with these myths. Fearing that they will trigger a rebellion, these parents often do not set appropriate boundaries for their child's emotional or physical safety. Worried that their child needs to "let out his feelings," they may let a tirade get out of control.

By refusing to limit the buildup of your child's tantrums and defiance, you send the message that this is an appropriate way to deal with anger. It is much easier to apply the brakes to a slow-moving train, rather than trying to stop an out-of-control locomotive. By being clear and careful with your limits early on, you can help your child stay in control.

Banishing the Myths

These myths may be operating within you and preventing you from Taming the Dragon. For example, depression and guilt may be stopping you from setting limits for your child. Or if you think your child is holding in a lot of anger, you may believe that angry outbursts are a sign of progress. Or you may be expecting too much of your young child and, in exasperation, be coming down too harshly with punishments.

Before you can establish new, constructive ways to handle anger, you will need to stop the myths. Choose the ones that you believe create trouble for you. Track yourself one weekend with the goal of catching yourself. Then just pause. Stop. Think. Look. Listen . . .

Success comes by recognizing and stopping old patterns from replaying over and over. Now you are ready to build new patterns and to solve problems in a climate of peace.

15

Creating New Patterns

By watching, listening and understanding how your old patterns contribute to conflicts, you have already begun to resolve your family's anger problem. The next step is to trace the steps that led to a recent argument or current conflict. You can do that in the following ways.

- *List the first signs of anger through to the explosion and beyond.* Include whatever everyone said or did, from the beginning to the end.
- *Ask your children for feedback.* Your teens particularly will be more than delighted to tell you about *your* many contributions to the problem. They may even tell you what *they* did to set you off! Younger children will enjoy helping you draw a Rage Gauge (explained in Chapter 18), to chart your family's pattern of escalation.

Once you know the patterns that set off eruptions, you are ready to Tame the Dragon. You will be better able to step away from the usual buildup. The following are suggestions to help you avoid your old anger patterns and keep your cool.

Give Yourself a Signal

Signals cue you to stop the old patterns. Talk to yourself. Some phrases that work well are "Here we go again," "Now's the time to stop," or "Keep your cool." Remind yourself that the first step to establishing new patterns is to stop the old ones.

Never underestimate the power of humor. The sillier the signal, the better the relief. Making fun of yourself will help you gain perspective that an argument is not the end of the world. Think about a favorite cartoon clipped from the paper. Replay in your mind a scene from a conflict-filled movie (*War of the Roses*, perhaps, or *Adam's Rib*,) or television show (Laurel and Hardy, the Three Stooges, or any shoot-'em-up Western or bang-up cartoon). Visualize yourself as the Wicked Witch of the West or as the evil stepmother in *Cinderella*. Imagine that "60 Minutes" cameras are rolling into your house and filming your rage in all of its ridiculousness. The point is, find a signal that works for you.

Reward yourself for using your signal. Enjoy your success as you step away from the familiar pattern of rising anger. By watching and thinking about where things go wrong, and signaling yourself to stop, you have won a major victory. Now you are ready to try a few simple strategies to break the patterns.

Take Time to Cool Down

Stop talking! Take a deep breath. Tell yourself, "I am not going to let the Dragon out this time." Take a break. By staying calm and in control of yourself, you can interrupt the pattern.

Easier said than done, you say? Won't my child just keep yelling and kicking? Won't my teen just keep arguing and trying to get me back into the fight? Of course, the old patterns, while destructive, are comfortable and automatic. At first, your child will try to goad you into jumping back into the battle—and it will be tempting to do so. But remember: You are responsible for breaking the patterns and Taming the Dragon. Work on staying calm, even if you need to separate yourself from your child for awhile.

By staying calm, you become an excellent example for your child. It is important for your child to hear you say, "I am too angry now. I don't want things to get more out of control. I am going to take a break for a while and calm down." Then do it and *quit talking!* Once you are calm, you can come back to your child and use the communication and discipline skills described in later chapters.

Examine Your Expectations

While you are calming yourself, think about what has just happened. Have you been stuck on one of the myths? Have you been using words or body language as weapons? What is your child trying to say? What does your child need to get back in control? What would help?

Having reasonable expectations will help most of all. Do not decide that every angry confrontation needs discipline or a deep discussion.

Often all you need is a way for all of you to cool down. The whys, moral reasoning, discipline, and communication can come a little later. Once you feel calm and positive, you can be much more effective in teaching your child to use the strategies in Chapter 17, "Teaching Children Self-Calming Strategies."

Then decide what is important in the conflict. Most arguments are about trivial issues that deserve no further attention. If this is the case, you can then step away from the fight, shift gears, and move on to something else. If, however, the issue is important to you or another family member, it will wait until later, when everyone is more receptive to talking calmly.

Create a Positive Climate

When you are calm, you are ready to help yourself and your angry child shift gears. With young children, humor, hugs, play, or new activities will work. Be bold. Take leadership. Let your child know that it's time to do something else for a while. If your child is still angry, he may try to pull you back into the fight. Ignore these attempts and proceed with your new focus.

Try to help school-age children relax. Choose a book, a game, or a TV show that your child particularly enjoys. Get some distance from the problem. Take a walk, go for a bike ride, or fix something good to eat.

A still-angry teen may be all too eager to put some distance between the two of you. Before she escapes to her room, let her know you love her. Be positive, affectionate, and clear in your direction to stop the fight. You are sending the message that no argument is worth hurting the family, and that each of you will have another chance to present your point of view when you are both calm.

For most children, a bear hug can work wonders to Tame the Dragon and reconnect. Your affection and love will come through, even if your child doesn't immediately respond.

Set Limits

Once you have stepped away from the conflict, your child may still try to follow the familiar patterns. Your first line of defense should be to ignore his attempt to fuel the fire, and to find something else to do. If your child persists, however, limits are in order. You cannot allow your child to hurt himself or others. You cannot allow your teen to verbally abuse you or others. Do not be afraid to set boundaries; the sooner you do, the better.

Tell your child, "All this fighting is hurting our family. I am going to be more calm and positive from now on. I want you to calm down, too. If you can, that will be great, and we can go on to do ———. If not, you need to do something right now to get back into control."

For fresh ideas about effective limits, you will find discussions of various discipline strategies, appropriate to each age, in Chapter 22.

The next chapter discusses two of the most common anger patterns in young children: whining and tantrums.

16

When Your Child Whines and Throws a Tantrum

Because whining and temper tantrums are the two most common first steps that children take on the path toward the Dragon of Anger, we've included a special chapter to deal specifically with them. First we look at how parents with King of the Mountain, Appeaser, and Queen of the Worried styles tend to deal with these behaviors. Then we consider more effective strategies.

How Parents Respond to Whining

Whining is obnoxious and makes most parents feel frustrated and angry. Parents will respond to their child's whining according to their own styles.

Appeasers, the conflict-avoiders, will try to ignore the whining. If the whining continues (as it probably will), they will give in and give the child what she wants so that she will stop whining. It should be no surprise that the child will whine again and again; she has learned that whining gets results. Finally, one day her normally mild-mannered Appeaser parent won't be able to take it any more and, out of the blue, will explode.

A King of the Mountain parent usually responds to whining by yelling and demanding that the child shape up—or else. The family anger pattern quickly escalates, and an eruption is likely.

The Queen of the Worried parent probably cannot decide what to do and so will whine with the child. Soon they are in perfect harmony, both complaining about something that *should* be happening their way. Neither can just let the conflict go; every nuance must be examined for meaning. The trouble is that no one is listening. The volume and screech level builds to a high-decibel, whining rage.

The strategies for parents to stop whining, no matter your style, are simple:

1. *Do not whine at your child. Do not acknowledge your child's whines.* Say, "I can't hear you when you talk that way. If you want to say what you *do* want in a nice way, I will listen."

2. *Take a break. Calm down.* Break your family's anger pattern by not responding emotionally to your child's whines. Don't let the whines push your "hot buttons."

3. *Think about what your child might need.* If your child responds to your prompts to talk calmly, that's great. If not, get involved in another activity, one that promotes humor or that soothes you both.

4. *End the discussion until your child is ready to come to you in a positive way.*

> Ten-year-old Simon was a bright boy whose teachers were struck by his talent for drama, debate, and leadership. At home, Simon's family loved to talk. Mealtimes were a stimulating arena of discussion. But when Simon did not get his way, he became a full-fledged pain in the neck, out-arguing and out-complaining anyone in the family. He would go on at endless lengths, exasperating his parents with his filibusters that began with logic and ended in whining. His parents resented feeling that they had to give in to Simon just to get him to be quiet.
>
> Finally his mom and dad decided that they had had enough. Simon was no longer listening to anything they said, even when they carefully couched their words within a well-reasoned moral debate. His parents hated his whining; even worse, they realized that they had started doing it, too. Wise parents, they knew they could not win if they stayed in the game. So they went on strike.
>
> Simon's parents told him that impassioned mealtime debates about science, politics, and similar subjects were fine. Even discussions about family rules and chore assignments were OK. But they would accept no more of Simon's whining and carrying on to get everyone to take his side.
>
> From now on, his parents would signal him when he had taken the first steps into his whining pattern. They would set their watches as a signal to themselves and to their son. Then they would say, "You have sixty seconds to stop the whining." During the sixty seconds, they would act as examples by listening and staying calm. At the end of the minute, if Simon was still whining, he would need to leave the table.

How Parents Respond to Tantrums

Although some of us can tune out whining, it is more difficult to ignore a temper tantrum. We may tolerate a two-year-old's tirade, because we understand that she is not yet able to tell us why she is angry and what she needs. But tantrums in an older child are especially exasperating and can be downright embarrassing. Many children have mastered the art of throwing a tantrum in public, knowing their parents will give in to avoid a scene. Adolescents are particularly sophisticated at raging when we will be most humiliated.

Parents will respond to their child's tantrums according to their different styles.

Appeasers are likely to give in too often. Their children generally have gained so much power and control through their tantrums that they no longer even have to stage a full-blown, screaming hissy-fit to get their parents to back down.

Usually these children run into problems with friends and adults outside the family who will not always give them their way. Their parents are generally surprised and have trouble taking action when teachers or other parents call to express concerns about these raging Dragons.

Queen of the Worried parents often respond to tantrums with lectures and shaming. Many of these children are frustrated and resentful of their parents' constant morality lectures and attempts to make them feel guilty. Worried parents do not show a confident, calm authority and are anxious about taking control. Tantrums give their children the power and control.

Rebellion becomes a way for the children to free themselves and establish control in a fight. Going on strike, refusing to talk or listen, seething with rage—some kids just become immovable. What is more powerful than a sit-down strike in the middle of McDonald's?

King of the Mountain parents may throw their own tantrums; it is sometimes difficult to tell who starts the tantrum. Yelling, stomping, fist-clenching, kicking, and hitting may quickly build from both sides. Everyone rapidly gets out of control, and the anger pattern grows darker.

Should you ignore a tantrum? Or should you set limits and stop the tantrum because your child may be hurting himself or others? You should do *both*—although you may be protesting, "But that doesn't make sense. How can I do both?"

The following are the steps to taming your child's tantrums:

1. *Ignore the tantrum.* Ignoring it gives you time to take a break and calm down. It is the first and most important step in Taming the Dragon. However, most parents find it impossible to stand there, watching their child throw a tantrum, and successfully ignore it. So instead, read a magazine. Go to the bathroom. Vacuum. Do something that will really distract you. You also will be showing your raging child that you truly do intend to break this anger pattern.

2. *Give yourself a time limit for ignoring the tantrum.* About five minutes for young children and ten minutes for school-age children is long enough. (You know about how long it should take your child to back down.)

3. *At the end of the time limit, set firm, clear limits for your child to stop the tantrum.* Let your child know, "It's time to settle down now. By the time I count to (you choose a number that makes sense to your child), I want you to be back in control."

4. *Be ready to discipline if necessary.* If, after the counting (or singing a silly song or playing a favorite tape), your child is in control, great. It's time for a big hug and words of praise. If your child is not in control, it's time for discipline. In Chapter 22 on discipline, you will learn how to choose a consequence appropriate for your child, perhaps a time-out, loss of privileges, or extra chores for each minute that your child continues to be out of control.

What to Do If the Tantrum Turns Dangerous

What if your child is really hurting himself, or you, or something in the house? This is clearly a dangerous time that requires attention to safety.

- First, try a solid hug as a restraint while saying firmly, "This must stop now."
- Give your child the count to be in control, as we just described.
- If he continues to struggle and inflict damage, immediately remove him to a safe, isolated place where he cannot hurt or be hurt.
- Do not talk when your child is resisting. Gently, but firmly, guide him to the calm-down, time-out spot. Then leave. Anything else you may try will make him fight harder.

The following example shows what one family did to cope with their child's tantrums in a positive way.

Molly was a strong-willed, active little girl. Her mother was a worrier, and her father had an explosive temper. The combination of the parents' styles meant that somebody was always upset or mad, or both, at Molly's house. She felt she had no way to take control, except to throw tantrums. As Molly reached school age, her rages became more intense and more frequent, until, at times, her parents felt virtually like strangling her.

They wanted the whole problem to stop and had even realized the most difficult part of all: that they were part of the problem. They were working hard to stop their roles in the family's anger pattern, but Molly just seemed to be getting worse.

Molly could not believe that her parents really were going to stay calm and handle anger problems differently now. Time and again, she put them to the test. Her tantrums grew longer and louder, as she tried to get her parents to follow her back into the old, familiar pattern.

Molly's parents decided that, when they ignored Molly, they would get a needed break to calm down and shift gears. But if they ignored her for more than a minute, Molly's tantrum exploded. They decided to set clear limits. If Molly wanted to have a tantrum, she had to go to the alcove behind the stairs, where her parents put a beanbag chair and some drawing materials for her to use to calm herself.

So that they wouldn't have to listen to their daughter's tantrum and be tempted to respond, the parents put on a CD and danced. They even found themselves laughing and enjoying their newfound release from the Dragon.

For each minute that her tantrum continued, Molly owed the family one minute of weeding in the garden. For getting back in control by the time her parents counted to ten, and for each time the family respected the cool-down signal, they earned points for a special time together. The best reward, however, was a big hug and the feeling of accomplishment. They had done it!

Do not feel that you have to suddenly rush through a gamut of new strategies to stop the whining and tantrums. Most important is learning to interrupt the pattern of conflict. By setting the example for a climate of calmness, you already have begun to change to a more positive style. When your child is sure she cannot push your buttons and call out your Dragon, you're on your way to establishing new, healthy patterns.

You will need more time to discover and understand exactly how the anger patterns build in your family, but keep watching and listening. As you learn more about the patterns, you can step away from them, stop the buildup, and focus on being calm and in control. Next, we'll present the tools to help you on your way.

17

Teaching Children Self-Calming Strategies

Children's anger becomes a problem in a family when it is too intense, too frequent, or too disruptive. To master anger, children must develop ways to calm themselves. When they know they can cool the rage building within them, they gain a sense of self-control, self-esteem, and mastery. This chapter focuses on teaching children ways to calm their own raging Dragons, with techniques and ideas for infants to adolescents.

Helping your child manage his or her inner tensions can help prevent the buildup of anger that leads to verbal and physical outbursts. By recognizing the subtle signs of tension brewing, you can interrupt the eruption process and help your child reduce his or her anger level or redirect it to more appropriate outlets.

Assessing Your Family's Natural "Rhythms"

Children will learn self-calming strategies best from parents who are sensitive to the family's particular anger patterns, so your first step is to examine the climate of your home. Ask yourself the following questions.

• *When family members come home tired and frustrated, can you count on peaceful interludes for reducing stress?* Are these interludes centered on your child? Some parents rely on a run after work to reduce their tensions after a rough day. What avenues do your children have?

They need relaxation times that are predictable, with a portion, but not all, of the time spent by themselves.

A nap is vital for toddlers *and* for parents who need a break from a busy two-year-old, but it should not be the only stress-free time during the day. Your toddler needs relaxation time with you, for stories, singing, rocking, and unwinding.

• *What can you provide for an older child, whose constant stream of activities may place demands on the entire family's time?* Some families respond with detailed schedules and heavily marked calendars. Others have a more chaotic, frenzied approach. Either way, many school-age children have little or no "free" time, to spend relaxing by themselves or in stress-free activities with their parents. You and your child are often on overload. Where are the havens from the pressures and frustrations?

• *Which activities bring both you and your child a sense of calm?* Develop them into a time you can share and a time for each of you to relax independently. Your styles will dictate your choices. Your routine will determine when you most need the wind-down time. Your newly peaceful interlude will provide a predictable period of calm, a time that you and your child can count on. Make this a top priority. Cherish the connections you build.

Strategies to Calm Children

Now that you've assessed the climate in your family, you're ready to begin teaching your child ways to manage his or her tension or stress.

Infant Soothers

Even in the womb, mothers can sense their baby's moods and arousal states. Often unconsciously, we parents begin subtle actions that bring quieting and calm. After children are born, as we tentatively respond to a cry or howl, babies let us know whether we have provided relief from their tension, hunger, or pain.

Babies train us to understand what they need: which touches soothe, which voices console, which actions help them reduce their own frustrations. Through this first, mutual communication, your baby develops the art of self-soothing. But if a parent is too invasive or too passive, the child cannot develop a sense of self-control.

> Angie was an active, alert, inquisitive baby. She loved rough play and excitement, yet would often end up overstimulated. Eager to help, her parents would try to rock and console her, but she would become even more fussy.
>
> At bedtime, Angie seemed to become especially active and alert.

When she cried, her parents assumed she wanted to be held. So she would cry longer, and they would hold her longer. But when they left her with a babysitter, she quickly would cry her lungs out, then sleep.

Her parents decided she must not be getting enough attention and became more intrusive at bedtime, trying to soothe her. At first she resisted, but Angie gradually came to depend on this nighttime ritual, which soon stretched into a two-hour marathon of story-reading, rocking, singing, cuddling, and more rocking into the night. By age two, Angie could not relax or sleep without an adult in the room.

Her parents had imposed on Angie's own ways to release tension (e.g., suppressing her bedtime crying) so that she had lost the chance to develop strategies for herself. At a time when she needed to develop independence and mastery of her body, Angie became more dependent on her parents. Her frustration and anger grew as she reached age three.

"Comforters" for Preschoolers

Preschoolers need ways to comfort and soothe themselves. It is no accident that the security blanket or special teddy bear is so important; it satisfies young children's need to comfort and control themselves. When preschoolers can meet these needs, they are ready to conquer more of their world: learning to dance, sing, color, build with blocks, ride the Big Wheel. These activities all involve intense, focused physical release and give children a sense of control and pride.

Instinctively, and with the peaceful interludes you have established at home, you can help your preschool child learn to relax at the first signs of anger:

1. *Begin to hum or sing as soon as your child begins to fuss over a frustrating task* (a button that won't fasten, for example). Your singing may distract and encourage your child to try again more calmly.

2. *Help your child find ways to cope independently with the many frustrating situations young children will inevitably face.*

3. *Become a guide and example, suggesting what your child might do to correct the problem and offering a sense of "I can do it myself!"* Trying to do it for your child will often result in more frustration, more resistance, and more anger.

4. *Remain calm and optimistic.* Use the techniques you have been practicing to keep your cool. Your anger will only increase your child's.

5. *Speak calmly.* Give your child a useful example to imitate. You can say, "Sometimes I feel angry, too, and I do ——— to help me feel better." Then start your own calming task and encourage your child to join you.

6. *Try to distract your child.* Many preschoolers respond to redirection. The distraction is most effective when it gives your child a chance

to calm herself. Suggest that the two of you reread her favorite story. Remind her that her stuffed animals might want to play. Place crayons and paper in easy reach.

  7. *Beware of trying to distract your child with treats and other indulgences.* These will only encourage your child to continue expressing anger inappropriately, in the hope that you'll offer a bribe again.

Calming Your School-Age Child

As children grow older, they need more time alone to cope. Time spent in their room can be a relaxing time for children to regroup, particularly if parents provide materials for comfort and consolation, such as books, tapes, art supplies, and favorite crafts. More active children may do better if they spend their "solo" time busily performing a chore or being allowed time for active play. These outlets are especially effective if you suggest them before your child has exploded. If aggressive or hurtful behavior occurs, discipline is necessary.

Do *Not* Let It All Hang Out. Faddish adult therapies have been built on the notion that humans bottle their emotions and that at times they need to release the tension, by screaming, perhaps, or hitting pillows, or enduring rough and pounding massages. Do anything to "get it out of your system"! However, there is no evidence that encouraging aggression in any way reduces problems with anger control. Indeed, plenty of data suggest that encouraging aggressive behavior may actually encourage aggressive tendencies.

  Some parents encourage their children to beat a pillow or hit a punching bag when they are angry. These children are using very aggressive actions while they are thinking angry thoughts, which may include blaming and revenge fantasies.

  It is never a good idea to allow children to behave aggressively, not even toward toys or other objects, when they are angry. Doing so takes away children's chances to develop more appropriate ways to release tension, such as sports, dance, a brisk walk or a bike ride around the block, vacuuming the living room, or scraping the peeled paint on the house. All of these provide a time for contemplation and help children cool off.

Relaxation Exercises. Many school-age children also respond well to relaxation exercises, the most effective of which have been developed by Elizabeth Stroebel, Charles Stroebel, and Margaret Holland. Their "Kiddie Quieting Response" offers the following active strategies that parents can teach to help children calm themselves:

  • *"Rag Doll":* The child flops, squirms and rolls, mimicking the loose, disjointed movements of a rag doll. Then, on a secret cue or code word, the child falls, limp and relaxed, so that, if you were to lift an arm, you would meet no resistance.

• *"Birthday Party"*: The child takes a deep, deep breath and slowly blows out the candles on an imaginary birthday cake. Then, peaceful and with eyes closed, the child makes a wish and imagines a happy thought. Use an image your child enjoys: blowing up a balloon, floating in an ocean of chocolate milkshake.

• *"Tense and Release"*: If you have taken an aerobics or yoga class, you know that muscles must be flexed and tensed before you can release them effectively. Patients with chronic back pain related to muscle tension also learn this technique. Biofeedback treatments for tension headaches, stiff necks and similar discomfort also use the tense-and-release principle.

• Although the tense-and-release technique sounds simple to teach, you will be most successful if you help your child "see" the exercise by imagining a favorite fantasy character or sports hero as a model, as in the following example.

> Billy was a turbulent child who drifted from helpfulness and sensitivity to distress and frustration. He would erupt in a tantrum if he could not do what he expected of himself. His mother became an easy target for his rage. While she tried to stay calm and keep her sense of humor, Billy would resist her attempts to set limits. He would yell even louder if she tried to sing silly songs to calm him, which had worked when he was younger.

> Billy's mother decided to hold a ceremony in which Billy was awarded a baseball cap emblazoned with "24," the number of Billy's baseball hero. Billy could wear the cap as long as he remained cool and calm.

> If he became upset, Billy would have to engage in a secret baseball ritual. He would flex his muscles and stand in various batting and fielding poses. Then, at the signal from his mother, he was to become instantly quiet and at peace, thinking of his next act of good sportsmanship or helpfulness.

> If he could then shift to a positive activity, he would be allowed to play or watch his favorite baseball video before dinner. If he did not choose to be positive and in control, he would lose his privileges. Gradually, Billy became a good sport.

Teens: Time Alone, Time on Their Own

Junior high and high school students face serious pressures, from increased academic and athletic demands, to anxiety about appearance, to worry over dating and friends, to opportunities for high-risk behavior. Home may become the pressure-release valve.

Your teen's rages may flare seemingly from nowhere. Emotional storms may seem to rain down on your family. If you feel helpless in the wake of this emotional turmoil, your teen has sent you an excellent signal about how he or she is feeling.

> *Erica had been a fussy youngster, anxious and easily upset. By adolescence, she had learned to cope by being super-organized and in control. When she entered high school, however, she felt overwhelmed by the mountain of pressures and could no longer keep up her efficient, confident image. She felt like a failure and feared that she would be publicly humiliated if the "real," vulnerable Erica were exposed.*
>
> *She saw any mistake as a disaster. If her parents pointed out that she had left her towel on the floor or missed doing a chore, Erica exploded. She began picking on her younger brother with vicious teasing meant to ridicule and expose his flaws. As the family conflict mounted, Erica often "won" the wars but lost more and more confidence. Could she really build herself up by tearing others down? Or was it time she learned to deal with her own stress and calm the rage inside?*

As they mature, most teenagers become better able to recognize their own increasing anger and tensions. They need safe ways to be separate from the family when they feel under stress. Competing in sports, talking to friends, even doing household chores can be constructive outlets for reducing tension.

Parent-Teen Contracts. If your teen has times when she is not yet ready to discuss her feelings and needs to get away to cool off, you might set up a contract between you. The contract should include the following elements:

1. *Agree on a set place for your teen to go for a set time.* Going to a friend's house, which might involve an active walk or bike ride, is a popular choice. The universal haven, of course, is the teen's own room.

2. *Agree ahead of time that, when your teen is on the verge of explosion, she can leave a note or otherwise signal her need for coping time.* Later, calmed and under greater control, she will be more ready for problem solving and conflict resolution.

3. *Your teen must return home on time and be prepared to discuss her feelings and the issues of concern.*

4. *If your teen does not follow the agreement, you must set consequences.*

Family Meetings Set Limits. Let's come back to Erica, the teen who had turned her family into a battleground because she had not learned to manage her own stress.

> *During a family meeting, her parents and her brother made it clear that they would no longer respond to Erica's provocations or rages. If Erica needed a listening ear, help with homework, or someone to shoot baskets with to relax, they would be available.*
>
> *However, Erica would be expected to wind down from school more constructively. She could choose sports, music, TV, a snack attack, or phone calls to her friends. If she did not choose a positive solution that she enjoyed, her parents would find a tension-reducing activity for her. There were plenty of grungy jobs that needed doing around the house. For every minute of her rage, Erica would be required to do ten minutes of extra chores.*

Peaceful coexistence is possible! From babies to teens to parents, we all need comfort and caring. Tension-reducing times to relax, recharge, and renew connections are a vital part of each family day. These breaks prevent explosions and conflicts from building.

Breaking away from each other when conflict starts to build gives us all a chance to calm and soothe ourselves. Then we can be ready to understand and solve the problems that triggered the Dragon's rage. To see how, read on!

18

A Rage Gauge to Track Your Family's Dragons

Children are intrigued by ratings and categorizations, particularly as their desire for order and learning grows. Your child can help you develop a ratings system that tracks the pattern of escalating arousal in your family to help cool off your family's Raging Dragon. This system, known as the *Rage Gauge*, will help each family member to use self-control. It will encourage all of you to become more aware of the patterns that result in flare-ups, arguments, and eruptions.

Designing Your Rage Gauge

Create your family's Rage Gauge together. See the following example and use these simple instructions:

- Draw a large thermometer, using a one-to-ten scale. "One" signifies a state of perfect calm. Each higher number reflects increased levels of anger.
- Along one side of the thermometer, write which actions, thoughts, and words you would use as you become increasingly upset or aroused.
- Along the other side, write the actions, thoughts, and words of your child's anger pattern.

YOUR FAMILY'S RAGE GAUGE

Mom & Dad		Your Child
	EXPLOSION!	
Dad shouts, Mom cries.	10	Throws, kicks, screams. Goes to room, locks door.
Pounds fist.	9	Slams door.
Voices raise.	8	Yells, curses, stomps.
Eyes flash. "*No!*"	7	Thinks: You never let me. . . . Argues
	6	
We repeat, louder.		"No! I want my way!"
	5	
	DANGER!	
	4	
We repeat . . .		"*WHY?*"
	3	"I demand . . ."
We repeat . . .		"I demand . . ."
	2	
Your child minds.		I get my way.
	1	
	PERFECT CALM	

Elementary school children will enjoy decorating the Rage Gauge. At the bottom, use pictures reflecting a state of family calm. At the top, a picture of a dragon breathing fire or a picture of Mom or Dad in a tizzy fit will underscore the message.

Using the Gauge to Talk about Your Anger Patterns

After creating your Rage Gauge, use it to discuss what it shows about your family's patterns. To help everyone understand how it works, use the Rage Gauge to chart a recent conflict. As you retrace the steps that led to the explosion, your child will see that you are part of the problem and part of the solution. First, show what you recognize as your own pattern of escalation. Then, encourage your child to think about how he becomes less calm and more angry. Particularly focus on the *actions* and *words* you each use that trigger a "heat wave" up the scale toward the explosion point. Discuss what you *do* in reaction to each other to increase the tension. Discuss what you *think* and what each of you *expects*, which increase the tension. (Of course, you must decide how much of this discussion is appropriate and relevant for your child.) Use the following questions to guide your discussion.

- What actions, thoughts, and words can you use to reduce the tension?
- How can each of you be responsible for stopping the escalation?
- If you stop your anger from rising, is the other person likely to stop, too? Or will he or she move to a higher level, to intentionally provoke you into conflict?

Guidelines for a New Pattern

Now you can use your gauge and discussion to put a new system into action with the following guidelines.

Find Your Threshold

As you retrace the conflict, determine the threshold point at which each family member *first* knew that he or she was beginning to get angry. Circle that number on the Rage Gauge in red, or mark it with a "Danger" sign. This is the point at which each of you can most effectively make changes. At a low level of arousal, we are all more capable of self-control, more able to use cool-down strategies, and more receptive to discussion. Once you've established your threshold, the family can do the following.

Choose a Code Word

Give this threshold point a name. The more involved your child is in choosing the name, the better. The name can be symbolic of anger: Code Red/ Dragon Time/ Watch Out!/ Fire! It can be a trigger for cooling down: Cool It/ Chill Out/Snowstorm. The allure of a secret word can be powerful. Whatever word your family chooses, it is important that you do not often use it in other contexts.

Respect the Code

All of you must agree to respect use of the code word. At any time, any of you can use the signal word if your own anger has reached the threshold level. Or anyone can use it if anger is rising in someone else.

Many parents worry that, in the heat of real conflicts, their children will not respect the signal. After a trial use on the honor system, you will probably find that your child is intrigued by the concept and will offer helpful modifications.

Most *parents* are the ones who have difficulty respecting the signal. Your child will signal you when you are lecturing, nagging, and disciplining, because these are the times when the tension is high. Although you may resist the interruption, remember that your child is taking the first step toward stopping the cycle of inappropriate anger.

Take a Minute of Quiet

When someone uses the code word, *everyone* must stop talking and stop moving for sixty seconds. During the minute of quiet, each of you is responsible for trying to relax physically and thinking calming thoughts.

Be a Model of Calm

Make staying in control your top priority. You can discipline after everyone is calm. For the minute of calm, however, you must be the model. Talking out loud helps: "I'm going to chill out." "I'll take six deep breaths." "Imagine me floating in a chocolate shake." Let your child hear the mind-control you are using to be calm.

At the end of the minute, the parent will say, "Are you calm enough to talk now?" If the answer is yes, you can hold a brief family discussion to decide if you can resolve the problem immediately or if you will need a later meeting to discuss solutions. If, after a minute of calm, everyone is not calmer, each of you must go to a separate room for some quiet time. Later, schedule a family discussion to resolve the issues. (See Chapters 19 and 20 for more ideas for structuring discussions about feelings and establishing problem-solving times.)

Practice the Signal

It is important to practice how you will use the signal in real situations. Play "What if?" Act out a typical buildup of anger. Let each person have a turn giving the signal and respecting the signal. Set some simple practice times for the first few days, being positive about even small steps that your child makes to use the plan correctly.

Be Clear about Consequences

Sometimes your child may try to use the signal to avoid punishment or to avoid having to take responsibility for his own behavior. Be clear from the beginning that, after the cool-down minute, discipline still will follow. At the end of the minute, you may be calm enough to consider a less-heated approach. At the end of the minute, your child is often more ready to comply and to apologize for misbehavior. Do not discuss the problem further unless it is truly negotiable *and* your child remains calm.

Most parents will not need to set negative consequences, beyond increased quiet time, for not respecting the code word. However, very aggressive children, with a long history of tantrums or control battles, may need more. You might develop a chore list and explain that, for each minute your child stays out of control, she will have to spend ten minutes doing chores. Other options include loss of privileges, restriction, offering restitution, or doing the chores of the person with whom she is angry.

Use Incentives

Set rewards for respecting the signal word and the minute of silence. Family rewards for shared activities are great. Older children may want to work for more time with their friends. Younger children may be thrilled to work for stickers. (Computer or video addicts may strive for more time on the computer or video game.)

Review Your Rage Gauge

After using the Rage Gauge for a week, hold a family meeting to review, refine, and revise it. Review the temperature markers and, if necessary, write more details about the behaviors, thoughts, and words that trigger a rise in temperature. You can make the cool-down process more relevant to your family's style, as long as everyone respects the code word. For example, making funny faces or shooting basketball free-throws may be good ways for you to "chill out" in your minute of quiet. Be creative. Do what works! Remember: Don't talk until *everyone* is calm.

Praise your child each time she respects the signal. Encourage her to be proud of her increased self-control. You might discuss your own difficulties in respecting the signal and what you did to stay calm. Keep your sense of humor and your spirit of optimism alive during these discussions.

After several weeks of the plan, you will probably start noticing that your family is using the code word much less often and that you are having far fewer anger outbursts. Set a target number to define your success (lowest number of outbursts in a week). When you have reached your goal, celebrate!

PART IV

STRATEGIES TO COMMUNICATE, DISCIPLINE, AND RESOLVE CONFLICTS

19

Talking to an Angry Young Child

The Dragon of Anger has many faces and shades, from purple rage, to pink indignation, to gray resentment. The Dragon's face you see in your family will depend on the age and temperament of your child—and on the face you see in your own mirror.

Teaching your child how to talk about anger and other emotions is one of your most crucial responsibilities as a parent. The model you provide and the way in which you share your own feelings will speak louder than any words. If you state your feelings calmly and respectfully, your child will learn to use this model. If you rant and rave when you're angry, your child will see that this is the norm.

Be Ready to Listen

The way you respond when your child talks to you about feelings is particularly important. Caring parents must establish a climate of understanding and acceptance when children confide feelings of hurt, sadness, disappointment, frustration, and anger. If you are too busy or distracted to respond, or if you dismiss or ignore your child, he or she becomes frustrated. Some children may become more withdrawn; others may become more active and rebellious in trying to draw your attention.

As you show your child you are listening, you must also teach him or her to listen to and consider other people's feelings. Listening does not necessarily mean giving in to unreasonable or inappropriate demands that sometimes accompany emotions. ("I want" does not always result in "I get.") Real communication begins with mutual respect.

Communication Skills to Use at Different Ages

When you know you and your child understand each other, you can begin the important task of compromise and problem solving. This process, a key to Taming the Dragon, can be applied throughout your child's life.

Communicate with Your Infant

Too often we assume that because children are not yet talking, they cannot understand language. Infants *do* respond both to our nonverbal and verbal communication with them. Consider how your baby would react to this situation:

> *Dad has rocked sleepy baby Andy and put him down for his nap. Five minutes later Andy begins screaming in his crib. Dad goes in to check on the infant and finds he has dropped his pacifier onto the floor. In a soothing voice, Dad says, "Oh, Andy is mad. He can't reach his pacifier. Hang on just a sec and Daddy will be back with Andy's nice clean pacifier." Dad quickly washes the pacifier in the bathroom and hurries back to Andy, whose crying has eased. Dad says, "Here's Andy's pacifier. Now everything's OK for Andy again. Now Andy can have his nap." Dad gently touches Andy's cheek with his finger and quietly leaves the room as the baby sucks peacefully.*

Most babies would sense that Dad's soothing tone is his message that he understands what the baby needs and will respond. But how would Andy have reacted if his dad had poked his head into the bedroom, checked to make sure the baby was in no danger, then snapped, "Why do you need that (expletive deleted) pacifier? Knock it off and go to sleep!"?

If you shout at a baby, you will leave him unconsoled and misunderstood. He may become more aroused, more agitated, and more frustrated because no one has understood his feelings or met his needs.

Each time you respond to your baby's cries and physical demonstrations of discomfort, you teach him that his expressions are important. He learns that others want to listen, understand, and help. When you rock him gently or change his diaper, you are showing him nonverbally that you care and understand, by providing soothing and relief. Your baby is too young to understand your words, but, with a sigh or a coo, you can begin the verbal process of labeling feelings. You can also encourage his first attempts at self-control by praising him, for example, when he uses his pacifier to soothe himself.

Communicate with Your Toddler

Between one and two years, children develop tantrums to express feelings and needs. No parent looks forward to them, but it may help to see these displays of temper as the child's instrumental attempts to gain something to satisfy herself. At this age, it is very important to *label the child's feelings*, state her needs, and give her a way to console herself. Satisfying her needs will reduce her arousal, of course, but that is not always possible or appropriate. She needs your help to learn self-control.

> *Two-year-old Jenny screams for the shiny cigarette lighter, which her mother has placed out of her reach. Jenny's "I feel MAD!" equals "I want." But, of course, her mother cannot console her by giving her the lighter. Mommy puts it away in a closed cupboard and hopes Jenny will forget about it. But "out of sight" no longer means "out of mind." The little girl screams louder. What can Jenny's mother do now?*

Now Jenny's mother is ready to teach Jenny her first self-control messages:

- She can tell Jenny that she cannot have the lighter because it is hot and it can hurt.
- She can offer Jenny a choice of safe toys, a soft ball, perhaps, or a favorite stuffed animal.

The toddler's "I feel ... " becomes "I am understood. I can't get what I want, but Mommy has told me why—and what I *can* play with." Jenny begins to understand that she has a choice about what to do to cope. She has learned her first self-control message.

Jenny should not be allowed to continue her tantrum and certainly should not be given the lighter. Even at this stage of development, children need limits set on unacceptable expressions of anger or coping strategies.

You can communicate the following messages to your toddler through your words and example:

- "When you feel, I will understand. When you show me in a calm way what you feel, it helps me to listen. When I understand, I will consider how to help you get in control and help you satisfy your needs."
- "I will not give in to your demands when you are out of control. When you are out of control, I will help you find ways to console yourself and to be responsive to my attempts at soothing."

Be clear about these issues. Help your child know how to express feelings in appropriate ways. Set specific limits. You will be laying important groundwork for later stages.

Communicate with Your Preschooler

"I want it! I want it NOW! If I can't have it, I'll be mad! If I'm mad, I'll show you! I will kick, scream, run, throw, pout and make Mommy's and Daddy's lives miserable! I know how to get what I want! I get mad; you give in."

Unfortunately, the preceding is the pattern we replay all too frequently with our children. In public, we often give in to our child's demands because we are embarrassed or afraid of making a bad situation worse. At home we may give in to tantrums because we are tired or frustrated. Or maybe we think our child cannot communicate in a more mature way. By giving in, we have taught our child an effective lesson in communication—*Actions speak louder than words. The louder the better. Physical force wins*—but this is hardly the lesson we want him to learn.

Preschoolers know how to say the words "happy," "sad," and "mad," but they tend to confine their communication of feelings mainly to physical actions. We interpret our child's actions to mean certain emotions and needs. When we misread the cues, our child's frustration grows. When we use simple "feeling words" to describe our child's actions, we are giving him a positive example of how to use language. Our communication model helps our child feel understood.

Don't Expect Your Preschooler to Explain "Why." "Why?" is the hallmark of a three-year-old's curiosity. Because we hear our child use it so often, we assume that she can both ask and answer that question. We look down at a furious little face and clenched fist and ask, "Why are you mad?" The typical response is "Because!" or "You made me mad!" Yet we expect our child to be able to offer explanations about why she feels a certain way at a certain time. We may even lecture that she should not feel that way.

You are asking the impossible if you expect your child to be able to explain *why* he feels as he does. It is a setup for disappointment for you and confusion for your child. It is natural to want and to expect your child to show you his feelings at this stage. Just don't expect him to do this with controlled, rational speech. Language at this stage is the means to an end; that is, its purpose is to satisfy the child's egocentric needs. Feelings are often just an extension of whether his needs are met or not met.

Give Your Preschooler Communication Cues. You can help your child know what is acceptable communication. The following messages serve as limits to curb your child's inappropriate physical expression of anger. They give cues about how to communicate in a way that is acceptable and constructive:

- "I can't hear you when you scream."
- "I won't listen to you until you tell me in a calm voice."
- "Tell me what you do want, not what you don't want."
- "You never get what you want when you throw a tantrum."

Once your child has accepted the cue to speak in a controlled tone of voice, you must be prepared to give him your undivided attention. Pay attention to his body language and actions, as well as to what he says. Repeat all or part of what he has said; this helps him to know he has been heard. By paraphrasing, you become a sounding board that helps him clarify his thoughts and gives him a springboard for expanding and explaining.

Teach Your Preschooler to Use Language to Solve Conflicts. At this age, children view feelings in black-and-white extremes. Happy or sad. Happy or mad. Happy or bad. *Sad, mad, bad*: Children put all three emotions at one end of their limited spectrum. To an adult, these words have quite different meanings, but to children they are all the same.

> Four-year-old Heather would play cooperatively with other children at her babysitter's house or at the homes of her friends. But when Heather's mother would let her invite a friend over, Heather would become whiny, bossy, argumentative, and rude. If she didn't get her way, she would scream, "I hate you!" When her mother would ask what she was feeling, she would become more out of control, make ugly faces, and yell that everybody was mean to her and made her mad.
>
> Heather's behavior was clearly "bad" when she broke household rules that she usually respected. Her exasperated mother would finally yell, "Cut that out or your friend is going home!" Heather would scream in protest, and her mother would ask her friend to leave. Soon after her friend had gone, Heather would settle down and play quietly in her room.
>
> Her mother couldn't figure out what was bothering Heather. During their bedtime talks she would ask Heather if she felt tired, hungry, jealous, angry, sad, rejected, or upset about something that she hadn't talked about. All the questions just seemed to make Heather's behavior worse. She began telling whoppers about the mean things her friend had done, which her mom knew could not possibly have happened. Heather's tantrums and screams of "I hate you!" increased.

To help Heather understand what she was feeling, her mom used the following steps, which you also can use to help your preschooler communicate feelings.

Set Limits First. Heather's mother decided that before Heather could talk about what she felt and what she wanted, discipline was in order. Heather needed limits and boundaries set for her. Mother made it clear that she would help and listen to Heather only if she used a calm voice. If Heather yelled, she lost a privilege and had a time-out. Meanwhile, Heather's friend would not be sent home but would be allowed to keep playing with Heather's special toys with Mother while Heather was in time-out.

Stop Speaking for Your Child. Mother also decided to stop intervening and jumping in to speak for Heather at the first sign of a conflict. She told Heather that she was confident that Heather was ready to share with her friend and solve disagreements by herself.

Role-play with Your Child. When Mother and Heather played dolls before bedtime, Mother began to set up brief conflicts between the doll friends. Mother would play an out-of-control doll and ask the other doll, which Heather played, for advice. Mother then guided Heather into a conversation of simple phrases and questions that she could use to solve the problem:

- "Let's quit fighting."
- "Can I have a turn with that toy when you're done?"
- "I'm mad right now. I need to play alone for a minute."
- "You take this toy and I'll take that one. Then we'll trade."

In the safe activity of play, Heather practiced her conversational and self-control skills. As her skills grew, she began using these statements and questions in real situations with her playmates. Heather could not yet fully express what she felt or why, but she was much more able to calm herself and to stop conflict from growing.

Don't Try to "Rescue" Your Child. Mother found that as she let Heather play more independently, Heather's anger subsided. Her mother's presence had fueled her anger. Maybe Heather was jealous of her mother's attentions to her friends, or perhaps she resented her mother's overintrusiveness and too-quick involvement to rescue her. Heather could not explain these issues to her mother, but she was old enough to develop language skills. She could use language to establish self-control and work out problems with her friend.

Communicate with Your School-Age Child

By the time your child enters elementary school, he has begun to master the ability to control his physical outbursts of anger. You have taught him that "I want" and "I feel" do not necessarily mean "I get." You have taught him that, if he wants you to listen, he must be calm and speak in a quiet voice. You have given him simple strategies for resolving conflicts. He is now ready to use language more effectively to establish self-control.

Both you and your child will recognize what triggers his anger. A lost prized possession. A broken video game. A friend who teases. Nagging him to do the chores. Now it is time to teach him that language is a very effective way to cope with situations that upset him.

Public embarrassment will be the first motivator. Angry tirades will not win friends or status for a school-age child. Only babies whine; only bullies are violent. Children earn power and esteem by being cool and calm, by letting everyone win. Kids can learn to be calm to save face and to look good—first with friends, then with you.

Teach Your Child
"I AM C-OO-L!"

Self-talk can help your child prepare for a stressful event, think about its impact, cope with her anger, make a plan for what to do, and evaluate the effectiveness of her behavior. It's cool to be calm. Your child can learn to remember: **"I AM C-OO-L!"** The acronym stands for:

I: It's coming. I need to get ready.
AM: About me: my thoughts, my feelings, my plan.
C: Calm. Cope.
OO: Ooh, what do I do?
L: Look back. How did I do?

Here's how "I AM C-OO-L!" works:

I: *It's coming. I need to get ready.* When a stressful event begins, we all use self-talk to size up what is about to happen. Negative self-talk ("Oh, no. I can't deal with this again." "That jerk! He has no right to do that!") tends to make us more angry and increases physical arousal. Positive self-talk can reduce arousal and prepare a child to cope. Statements like these prepare a child for stress or provocation:

- "I can handle this."
- "I know this will upset me, but I've handled it before."
- "I won't let him bother me this time."
- "Just stay cool."

AM: *About me: my thoughts, my feelings, my plan.* When the stressful trigger begins, many children simply react with physical signs of anger. Your child can learn to think about how she wants to react. First she must know where she stands:

- What is the problem?
- What do I feel? What do I want?
- How do I explain what I'm feeling or what I need while respecting the other person's rights?
- How do I listen to what the other person is trying to say to me?

Your child gains control by taking the time to think through what is happening.

C: *Calm. Cope.* The older child can learn to be aware of the signs of increasing physical arousal. He can monitor himself inside as his "feeling temperature" soars. He can think:

- "I must really be getting annoyed. My palms are sweating and my fists are clenched."
- "I'm yelling now. I want to hit something!"

Self-talk about his arousal helps your child identify what is happening and gives him a signal that it's time to use coping strategies. The most effective and easiest coping tools are the physical relaxation techniques discussed in Chapter 17, "Teaching Children Self-Calming Strategies."

Your child can also use verbal cues to get under control. He can say quietly to himself:

- "I need to stay cool."
- "Just relax."
- "It's no big deal."
- "Settle down; don't make a fool of yourself."
- "Imagine I'm drinking a chocolate shake and I don't have to deal with this just yet."
- "Take a deep breath."

Besides cuing herself to stay calm, your child can also develop elaborate fantasies to help herself regain a sense of control. She can learn to use verbal and visual imagery to transform herself to a state of calm and a different frame of mind as in the following example.

Carrie's friends loved to tease her, because they knew they could count on her to fly into a rage, crying and carrying on until she finally stomped off in a huff. She was great entertainment on a boring summer day. But this time when they started to bait her about her red hair, Carrie didn't say a word. She just stood still, silently singing the words to a popular TV commercial and imagining herself, cool and grinning, floating in a huge bowl of her favorite ice cream.

When Carrie didn't react with her usual tantrum, her friends lost interest in the teasing and resumed their game. The message in Carrie's fantasy is clear: *Stay cool; you win.*

OO: *Ooh, what do I do?* Your child also can learn to use self-talk to figure out a plan of action. She can define her own feelings and needs and imagine the feelings and needs of the other person. If she's not sure, she can rehearse questions that might help her to see the other person's position more clearly. She can think:

- "What did my friend want the last time we had a fight like this?"
- "If I were in his place, what would I want?"
- "I know if I listen to him, he'll stop and listen to me."
- "If I try to focus on what I want *and* what he wants, we'll get along a lot better."

After she has thought about the other person's side, she can say: "Maybe we're both right," or "Let's decide together what to do about it." These types of statements can set the stage for each person to be heard and all viewpoints to be considered. *"How can we both get what we want?"* becomes an important part of the plan.

When your child is angry at or in conflict with another child, it is important to leave as much as possible of the actual plan up to her. If you supply the answers for resolving the problem, you take away your child's pride in finding the solution.

Your role is to successfully prompt your child to discuss her plan and use it. You can do this most effectively by being a good model yourself. After all, we all make mistakes. Get in the habit of letting your child hear you think out loud when you are angry or have conflicts. Talk about what you're doing to calm down. Tell her your plan for resolving the conflict. Your own self-talk will help you be in better control and show your child how to resolve problems.

L: *Look back. How did I do?* After he has settled a situation, your child can use self-talk to praise himself for his accomplishment. Even if the problem was not completely settled to everyone's satisfaction, praise your child for at least one aspect of his plan that was positive and in control. Ask your child to comment on what he thinks worked for him. Even if he says, "It could have been a lot worse," you can still turn this into positive feedback by helping him think about whatever went right.

Feedback is also a time for constructive planning. Don't tell your child, "You should have done this." Instead, ask him what he may want to try next time.

You might offer a model, an idea for a future plan of action, by introducing your suggestion with, "This is what worked for me when I was your age and had a problem like yours." Children would rather hear stories than lectures. Your story will be especially effective if you also note the mistakes *you* made in the similar situation and describe what your child has done to avoid those mistakes. Remember to keep the story focused on your child, rather than on yourself.

"I AM C-OO-L" can work for you and your child. Remember, it will take months to really master this skill, because it requires cool-down, self-talk, and problem-solving techniques.

Start with small steps. Play "What if?" Practice as you eat dinner or ride in the car. Reward your child for using one step at a time. Plan a celebration for when each of you has successfully used "I AM C-OO-L" with a family member or friend.

The communication skills you have learned in this chapter will take you far along the path to Taming the Dragon in younger children. In the next chapter, we'll look at techniques to help you talk to your teen.

20

How to Talk to Your Teen

You might assume that, because teenagers talk so much, they must be great at sharing their feelings. The truth is that most teenagers are terrified of revealing much about themselves, because they are afraid other people will ridicule or reject them. The following tips can help you communicate with your teen.

Talk in the Third Person

Adolescents often use anecdotes about their friends, movie clips, or other indirect strategies to discuss issues. Talking in the third person can be an effective way of communicating with them, as the next example illustrates.

> Fourteen-year-old Zach and his mother were doing the dinner dishes together. "How'd school go today?" his mom asked. Zach dried a plate, then said, "This kid in my English class cheated on a test today."
> "How do you know he cheated?" his mother asked.
> Zach slammed a fork into the silverware drawer. "I just know. OK?"

When you recognize a parallel from the third person to your teenager's life, be cautious about stating it. Continue the analogy as long as you can. If the story is really about your teen, the third-person format will give him a safe way to talk about whatever is bothering him.

Zach's mother recognized that Zach was telling her something important, but she wasn't sure exactly what he was trying to say. Had Zach himself cheated? Was he considering cheating? She knew she couldn't ask him outright; he would deny it or go up to his room in silence. Instead she asked calmly, "What do you think might have made this kid cheat on the test?"

"The teacher's a jerk!" Zach said vehemently. "He never tells us what to study for, and he doesn't explain the stupid grammar rules we're supposed to learn."

Zach's mother was listening carefully. "That sounds really frustrating and confusing," she said.

"It is," Zach said eagerly. "If anybody tries to ask the teacher anything, he just says, 'Do the practice sentences at the end of the unit.' Yeah, right. Like we really know how to do the sentences when we can't even figure out what the directions mean! No wonder that kid cheated. What else was he supposed to do?" He looked at his mother, who saw the question in his eyes.

Ask "What If?"

The third-person distance provides your teenager a stage for practice. By imagining other people's thoughts, feelings, and potential actions, he can think of options that might work for him or evaluate a choice he has already made. You can help by introducing a game of "What If?" in which you can offer constructive and even ridiculous options for your child to consider. He learns by weighing and evaluating others' real or hypothetical courses of action.

"Well," Zach's mom said slowly, "maybe there were other things he could have done besides cheating. What if he asked to talk to his teacher after class?" Zach rolled his eyes. "Or," his mother continued, "what if he asked a friend—preferably an 'A' student—to help him study for the test?" Zach smiled.

"Or what if he told his parents he had a problem with the class? Maybe they could have helped him come up with some other solution besides cheating. What do you think?"

"Yeah," Zach said doubtfully. "I guess. But what if his parents make a big deal out of his getting good grades?"

Zach's mother took a breath and let it out slowly. In her calmest voice, she asked, "Has something like this ever happened to you, honey?"

Zach put down the dish towel. "Yeah. It has."

Be a Good Listener

Once your teen makes the move to communicate more directly, he is ready for you to be a receptive listener. Try to hear his message. Do not evaluate, agree, or disagree. Simply echo and paraphrase what he says. If it's a loaded issue, such as cheating in school, and your teen is blaming and accusatory, be clear that you feel attacked. Ask for more constructive feedback.

Encourage Your Teen to Use "I Messages"

The formula for "I messages" is: "I feel ———— when ————." They seem simple but are difficult to do. State only what you feel without blaming or placing responsibility for feelings. The *when* has to be free of accusations. *When* describes time and place; *when* should not be provocative. The tone should be clear that each person is responsible for his or her own feelings.

The best way to get "I messages" from your teen is to start sending them. We parents are often so busy in our authoritarian role with teenagers that we stop being human and vulnerable with them. Show them how to take risks. Share your feelings with "I messages." Ask to be understood.

> *Zach and his mother sat down together at the kitchen table. Mom said, "Remember that college professor I told you about, who gave me an 'F'? I felt humiliated when he refused to answer my questions. I felt like quitting the master's program, but you and Dad told me to hang in there and get my degree. I guess you feel that way, too, sometimes."*
>
> *Zach said, "Yeah, Mom. I just feel overwhelmed when I have so many other pressures right now."*

This is not yet the time for discussions about what to do. First both of you need to be heard and understood before you can do something about the conflict. "I hear you. I know you heard me. Our positions are clear. Now what do we do about it?"

> *Mom said, "Well, when I was having problems, you told me to work with the other students to get that professor to listen to us. What are the other kids in your class feeling about this? Can you rally together?"*
>
> *Zach said, "I've been feeling all alone. I guess I should check*

*things out. I'll see if somebody can tutor me. Or, if everybody else is
struggling, we can all take a stand and get the teacher to help us."*

Teach Your Teen the Steps to
Problem Solving

Now that you've learned some tips about how to communicate with your
teen, its time to teach him or her about how to solve problems. Adolescents are ready to be responsible for settling conflicts and resolving feelings, if someone will teach them how. By teaching teenagers the steps of
effective problem solving, parents are giving them a tool they can use to
Tame the Dragon throughout their lives in both intimate and work situations.

In problem solving, it is vital to *avoid placing blame for the problem.*
"Who started it" and "why" simply make everybody angrier. Focus on
what your teenager can do now to move forward. Don't try for the one
"right" way. The best way is not "my way." Try to help your teen consider
various options that will meet the needs of all the people involved.

> *Scott, 16, and Kelly, 14, brother and sister, were in a state of constant
> conflict. They argued at the breakfast table, on the school bus, in front
> of the TV, and at all points in between, screaming, cursing, and sometimes slapping or kicking each other. Each believed revenge was fully
> justified.*
>
> *Personal space was their biggest battle issue. Scott was furious
> whenever Kelly used his blow dryer and forgot to return it. To retaliate,
> he would take all of her makeup out of the bathroom and throw it
> onto her bedroom floor. Kelly hated it when Scott would come into
> her room and take paper and school supplies without asking. And
> when he used the last of her hair mousse without telling her, she
> slammed him with her fist.*
>
> *These teenagers had never learned to settle their own differences
> and expected their parents to referee their fights. Each had become a
> tattletale. If their parents sided with one, the other plotted revenge.
> Their parents had grounded the teens so often and taken away so
> many of their privileges that life at home had started feeling like jail
> time, with the kids as prisoners and the parents as wardens. Was
> there any way to stop the constant fighting and help these teenagers
> solve their own conflicts peacefully?*

In the beginning, especially when the situation is as intense as in
the preceding example, it may be best to *follow a clear plan,* so that
problem solving moves forward in an orderly, rule-governed way. Later,

as you and your teenager become more successful, you can become more flexible.

> *Scott and Kelly's parents called a truce, then sat down with their teenagers for a family meeting. The parents made it clear that they would not referee any more conflicts. The two teens were mature enough to handle their own disagreements. If any more screaming, hitting, or destruction of property occurred, both Scott and Kelly would be considered responsible—no matter who "started" it—and be required to do extra household chores. If they complained, more work would be added. However, if they could successfully show that they were using problem-solving strategies, then their parents would reduce their chore load. Now the teenagers were ready to learn the problem-solving plan.*

Following are the steps Scott and Kelly's family used and that you can also use to teach effective problem solving. To help your family get started, you can use the worksheet on the next page as a guide, or create your own.

A Family Problem-Solving Plan

1. Define the Problem. Choose just one issue to resolve. State each person's view. Include each view within one definition of the problem. Keep it simple. Keep it positive.

> *Scott and Kelly were both conscious of the need for privacy and protection of their own space and possessions. They defined the problem as how to maintain respect for their privacy and belongings.*

2. Develop Options. Brainstorm ideas that will help solve the problem so that each person wins. This may mean that each person must lose, sacrifice, or compromise to have a more important need met. At this idea phase, *don't evaluate or defend positions.* Simply write down each option. Try to come up with at least three. Lighten up; silly options are OK.

> *The options Kelly and Scott proposed were:*
>
> *Option A: The two teenagers would never borrow from each other or go into each other's room;*
> *Option B: They could borrow or trespass only if they submitted a written request and obtained permission;*

FAMILY PROBLEM-SOLVING
WORKSHEET

PROBLEM DEFINITION: _____

Solutions   *Positive Benefits*   *Negative Results*

OPTION A:

_____

_____

OPTION B:

_____

_____

OPTION C:

_____

_____

OUR FAMILY'S SOLUTION CHOICE IS: _____ .

_____ will do _____ at _____ If done,
   (Who)   (What)   (When)

_____ ; if not, _____
     (Reward)   (Fine)

Signed _____ Date _____

_____ Length of Plan _____

_____ Review Date _____

_____

Option C: The teens would make a community supply closet and stock it so that more than enough of the prized toiletry items would be available. Whoever took the last of a product would write it down on the shopping list for purchase.

3. Evaluate Each Option. Each person must state the positive and negative aspects of each option for her- or himself and for the other person. No bargaining, lobbying, or persuasion is permitted at this point. The focus is on how various choices will satisfy and affect each person involved in the conflict. List the positives and negatives of each option.

Secretly, the parents preferred Option A for its simplicity and separateness, but they were careful not to impose their preference as the right one. They asked Scott and Kelly to list the good and bad points of each choice.

4. Throw Out Options. Eliminate any choices that have a relatively high number of negatives for one person, or are clearly unrealistic or unfeasible.

The two teenagers threw out Option B (written permission to enter each other's room) as too much of a hassle to consider seriously.

5. Choose an Option. The choice that offers the most positives and fewest negatives for each person is likely to become the clear winner. If not, you may need to go back to step 2, be more creative, and develop more choices.

Scott and Kelly chose Option C (the stocked supply cupboard) because it had the most positive aspects for each of them. Their parents accepted it, even though this choice meant additional purchases for them.

6. Write Down the Choice. Be specific. Who does what when? How will you decide if the plan is working? When will you change it if it is not? What will the consequences be if one person reneges on the agreement? What will the rewards be if both of you follow it? Be detailed. Write it all down.

Kelly and Scott put their agreement in writing and set consequences for not respecting its terms: If one entered the other's space to take an item, the violator would have to do the other's chores for two days.

7. Sign the Agreement. Make a public commitment. Post it. Look at it daily. Motivate yourselves to change, to follow through. Keep your word.

The teenagers set a time to reevaluate their agreement, then signed and dated it. They even posted it on the refrigerator. Their parents added an incentive: If there were no blowups for a week, the teenagers would get reinstatement of their phone privileges, which had been taken away during previous battles. This bonus helped Kelly and Scott to respect the agreement until the revision date two weeks later. At that time, the teenagers decided to go on the "honor" system and negotiate solution of another problem.

8. Give It Time. Stick to your commitment until the review date. Family problem solving works! But it takes time. It succeeds because you tackle one well-defined goal at a time.

9. Be Proud of Your Accomplishment! At your review date, focus on what went well. Revise and renegotiate if this problem still needs work. If you had success, celebrate. Then tackle a new problem. Success will come with one problem solved at a time.

Teens relish the control given to them with family problem-solving meetings. Parents welcome a positive structure so that teens can prove they can handle the responsibility of solving their own problems. With this format, everyone wins! Once you have success at home, both you and your teen will be calling meetings to problem-solve with friends and coworkers.

Now that we've explored ways to talk to your child when coping with the Dragon, the next chapter gives some insight into when talking is *not* always the first strategy to use when tension levels are high.

21

Sometimes the Dragon Needs Silence

KNOW WHEN TO *STOP* TALKING

Parents often need to respond immediately to a child's angry outburst. Sometimes, however, talking about what triggered the feelings and trying to solve the problem can be inappropriate and even destructive.

What to Do When the Tension Level Is High

When you and/or your child are highly charged, trying to discuss what's wrong might make you both feel angrier and more frustrated. Communication is important, but only *after* each of you is calm and willing to work things out. Use the following suggestions during high-stress situations.

Be a Model for Your Child

Your positive self-talk will help both of you cool down. Do not demand that your child get under control; this might just make her more confrontational. Instead, talk aloud about your attempts to be calm. Count to ten, practice deep breathing, or try one of the following self-statements:

- "I need to get back in control."
- "I'll be ready to listen once I settle myself."
- "I'm making a mountain out of a molehill. Once I take a break, I'll be more able to talk."

If your child does not respond to your model and is still out of control, discipline is in order. Say as little as possible when you discipline so that you don't fuel the Dragon.

Open the Lines of Communication

Remember, none of us appreciates being attacked or blamed. When you and your child are calm, always acknowledge your responsibility in an angry conflict. Apologize to your child for your part. Tell him how you will stay in better control in the future. Your child will learn from you that it is important to be conciliatory while being responsible.

Help Your Child Be Clear and Positive

Tell your child to be clear about what she wants so you can help. In times of frustration, parents often hear only a barrage of whiny complaints about what their child does not like or want. For example, in the heat of an argument about whether she can go to her first dance and stay out past curfew, a teenager is likely to haul out all the old guilt-induction tactics:

"*You* never *let me do anything fun! Other parents* always *let their kids do more than you let me do! You* should *come out of the Dark Ages; it's almost the twenty-first century!*"

Rather than whine back or, worse, begin Lecture #5931 about what a responsible parent you are, be a good model and open the lines of communication. *Be clear* with your teen: "I can't respond to what you *don't* want. Tell me what you *do* want."

You and your child will be much more able to really talk and hear each other if you erase three words from your vocabularies: *always, never,* and *should.* These words create a climate of defensiveness. They set the stage for the cycles and patterns of anger to breed and escalate.

Try to use "I messages" yourself. Be positive about what you do want, instead of stating what you don't want. "I like a clean kitchen when I cook. I know you have been busy today. I would like you to empty the garbage now. If you can, great. If not, I will take fifty cents off your allowance."

Give Your Child Feedback

Use "I messages" to let him know that you have feelings, too, and his behavior can hurt. Be clear that you want to hear him, but it was the negative way he was speaking that was unacceptable. "I feel attacked and like a bad dad when you yell and call me a jerk. I can help you better if you talk to me more calmly, like you do when you talk to your friend."

Give your child a chance to state his feelings, needs, and position constructively. Be respectful and positive in the way you respond. Focus on the appropriate aspects of his message.

Be Clear about What You Will Do and Why

If your child's needs and position are acceptable, tell her you are considering her position *because* she acted responsibly in the way she communicated with you. If you are open to negotiation, set a time and place for problem solving. If what your child wants is unacceptable, be clear that it is nonnegotiable.

Many families fight the same battles over and over because parents fail to be clear about limits and rules. There are many *nonnegotiable* rules that parents simply set and enforce with discipline. It is a good idea to list nonnegotiable rules and their consequences, so there are no surprises.

For Nonnegotiable Issues, *Stop Talking*

Further discussion creates the illusion that you will negotiate. It frustrates your child and increases his anger. It increases the odds that one or both of you will blow up.

The hardest task for most parents seems so simple: Be quiet! Do something else to signal that the discussion is over. Play your saxophone. Take a shower. Talk can come later when you are both calm, if a new negotiable issue arises. As you become more confident in using the discipline techniques in the next chapter, you will have less need to talk.

22

Setting Limits
on the Dragon

DISCIPLINE TECHNIQUES
THAT WORK

We all need to get our anger out in the open at times. But how can parents know when to encourage their children to express their anger and when to punish explosions of rage? This chapter offers guidelines and practical recommendations for typical discipline situations, beginning with a focus on positive methods of discipline. You will learn strategies and techniques, appropriate to your child's age and temperament, for handling a range of anger-related problems.

Discipline helps motivate children to express their angry feelings appropriately. Many parents forget that the most effective method of discipline is the *positive incentive*. If you aim your discipline mainly toward punishment, you may be unknowingly adding to your child's anger and frustration, and raising the likelihood of control battles. By using positive methods whenever possible, you will be motivating your child to change and mature.

Positive reinforcement refers to any consequence that follows a behavior and causes that behavior to increase in the future. Consequences can be material rewards, attention, or a favorite activity. You can use these incentives, not as manipulative bribes, but as ways to increase your child's self-control. Certainly, it is best to avoid lavish gifts and never-ending treats; they probably would work, but your child might soon decide that the only time she will behave appropriately is *after* she has asked, "What will you give me if I be good?"

The most powerful, yet subtle, positive consequences are the nonverbal rewards you give your child—a smile, a hug, an approving nod of the head, and careful attention to what your child is telling you. The power of listening is profound, particularly if you listen when your angry child talks about her feelings in a controlled way.

Listening to your child does not mean having to agree with his reasons for, or ways of expressing, anger. Listening means hearing him out, considering his side, and letting him know his views and needs are important.

Positive Reinforcement
with Preschoolers

When infants and toddlers show anger, parents often respond with quiet concern and nurturing. If you can use a similar technique with your three-year-old by focusing on one appropriate element of his outburst, you will be miles ahead. Always try to recognize the early warning signs that the Dragon of Anger is lurking. Respond to the positive signals and encourage your child to use them. The following example illustrates how a parent can do this.

> Alex was so proud of his ability to ride his trike. He would circle round and round—until he was cornered and could not back up. Then he would grunt and squirm, calling for help. When his mother came to his rescue, Alex would get angry because he could not do it himself. Then the tantrum would start.
>
> At first, Alex's mother would say that if he did not stop crying, he would lose his trike for the day. Alex would wail and bang the beloved trike into the wall, which just raised his own anger and frustration—and his mom's.
>
> Later, his mother became more observant about what was frustrating Alex. At the first signs that her son was getting stuck in the corner and calling for help, she would say, "Alex, I like it when you call me, and I understand it's hard to make it around this corner. I would be a much better helper if we could work together. Can we think of a traffic signal to use before you get to the corner, so I can come right away?"

Alex and his mother devised a traffic diverter that kept him from circling deeper into the corner. When he passed the diverter, Alex would ring the bell on his trike once if he was calm and in control, twice if he was getting frustrated and could use Mom's (the traffic cop's) help in steering, and three times if he was so angry that he needed to stop and do something else.

Mom praised Alex for using these signals and provided positive attention by "pretending" with her son while defusing and redirecting his frustration. She established a structure and provided an incentive for Alex to track his own anger and to express his feelings and needs more appropriately. When the bell rang, it was easier for Mom to intervene with praise for Alex's self-control. Most important, when Alex asked for help at the number-two signal, Mom had an opportunity to listen and attend to Alex's discussion of his needs.

Positive Reinforcement with School-Age Kids

It is crucial to focus on your child's positive actions when you're offering feedback. None of us responds well to "Yes, but . . ." or "That was great— why can't you do that all the time?" When you combine criticism with praise, your child will "hear" only the criticism.

> *Kevin, age 10, was bright and curious, but he had struggled with school from the beginning. His parents tried tutoring him, but their help just seemed to make him more frustrated. Homework time soon became a nightly battle. Kevin would get angry and resist his parents' suggestions for how to improve his work. Even when they offered more TV time if his grades improved, Kevin balked.*
>
> *His father was a meticulous man who took pride in a neat, orderly approach to life. He was especially frustrated by Kevin's disorganization and apparent lack of concern. He did not recognize the intense pressures he was placing on his son. When Kevin finished a spelling list, his father would focus on the one word spelled wrong, or the sloppy handwriting.*
>
> *Kevin's mother sensed Kevin's brewing anger. She would encourage him to take breaks from his homework when he began to sigh and hang his head. Her reviews of his work focused on which parts he had done well and the considerable effort he had made. She let Kevin's teacher handle the correcting and grading. Kevin's father soon became concerned about Kevin's growing dependence on his mother for homework help and his son's continuing resistance to "getting his act together."*

Kevin and his parents agreed that he would feel prouder of himself if he could work for longer periods on his own. They began to schedule his breaks a bit further apart each time. During the break, Kevin would review his own work for positive points. His father listened carefully as Kevin talked about the good work he had done, and recorded in a notebook the length of time Kevin had worked and the success he had had.

This technique satisfied the father's need for order and Kevin's need for his dad to provide quiet, supportive listening.

If Kevin felt angry or frustrated, he wrote his feelings in the notebook and took a break. Each week the family reviewed the log and praised Kevin's increasingly long periods of work. They discussed Kevin's attempts to control his anger and listened to his plans for the coming week. They let his teacher handle the job of correcting and grading. His parents quickly realized that Kevin did not need a TV reward; he was basking in their support and attention.

Positive Reinforcement with Teens

Parents may be so eager to help their teen through a difficult time that they may try to force communication. Learning not to "push" teens is important in Taming the Dragon.

> *Nick's girlfriend broke up with him last week and now was dating his best friend. Nick's mother was sure that her son must really be hurting—but every time she tried to get him to talk about his feelings, he told her to leave him alone. Nick says she doesn't understand anything about his life. Yesterday he even shoved her away from his bedroom door when she came to talk.*
>
> *"I don't know which way to go," his mother said. "Should his dad and I ignore his explosions because he's feeling so bad? Should we punish him for his awful rudeness? Isn't there some way we can help him understand that, no matter how angry or hurt he is, he can't just stomp all over other people's feelings?"*

Nick's parents felt cut off and rejected, yet they so wanted to help. The more they tried to get close, the more explosive Nick became as he pushed them away. They wanted to punish him for being so aggressive, but they also considered how much Nick was hurting.

Because their most important goal was to help Nick talk about his hurt and deal with his anger, they decided to focus on positive discipline.

> *First, Nick's parents both warned him that further aggression would result in extra chores and loss of privileges. They then stepped back and gave Nick space and privacy to heal the wounds from the loss of his girlfriend. They told him they would be there to talk when and if he was ready. When Nick came to them with even minor issues, they gave him their undivided attention. They insisted on being treated politely and made Nick's car privileges contingent upon treating them cordially.*

The hardest part of this discipline plan was not pushing Nick. His parents had to trust that he needed to work out his problems on his own, and that he would come to them if they remained calm and open and focused on positive incentives.

Other Positive Discipline Techniques

The Power of "Grandma's Rule"

"Work before play" was Grandma's rule, and it is still valid today. You can adapt it to help your child Tame the Dragon, by repeating, *"Before you get what you want, you must be positive and constructive in the way you express anger. If you are positive in the way you show your anger, we will respond with understanding and support."*

For younger children, you can say, *"Unless you tell me in a nice way, you will not get what you want."*

Children of all ages respond to this informal, yet all-encompassing wisdom. We often overlook its power. Think of all the times you have given in to tantrums and violated its spirit.

Whenever you offer a tantrum-throwing child candy in the supermarket or an extra story at bedtime, you have broken Grandma's Rule. Even if you do this infrequently, you are providing a powerful incentive for your child to express anger inappropriately. If you generally do not give in to the bedtime temper tantrum, but once or twice a month you are so tired that you give in and read an extra story, your child will learn to fuss longer and throw a harder tantrum.

If you try to establish a reward system or another behavior-change program after your child has gotten set in this pattern, be prepared for difficult times. Your child will likely show more severe tantrums and angry outbursts for a few days. It will take more time for her to realize that the previous reward isn't going to come again. Children with this pattern particularly need an intensive incentive system to establish appropriate behavior. Simply ignoring the tantrum will not be effective. It will be crucial for you to set up a constructive, positive system for her.

Incentive Systems

Star charts, checklists, incentive contracts—all of these systems can motivate children effectively. Even three-year-olds can respond to simple incentive systems. Teens thrive on them. The key to the system is targeting one behavior at a time and focusing only on positive goals and positive behavior. For example, you may be tempted to set a "no yelling" or "no hitting" goal for your young child, but she will have more success *starting positive behavior* than trying to stop negative behavior.

The following are suggestions for beginning an incentive system for your child:

1. *Let your young child know it is OK for her to be angry, as long as she states her feelings in a calm, quiet voice.* Make it clear that she will not get what she wants through tantrums.

Have her draw a picture of herself being calm and in control in a situation that usually triggers a tantrum or rage. Let her know she can put a sticker or a smiley face on the picture each time you catch her expressing anger in a calm way. Be lavish in your praise and affection when you see her doing this, even if she remembers only while she is practicing her new behavior with you.

2. *Let your child choose special activities or games with you as he earns stickers.* Be sure not to start a pattern of buying extra treats and toys. Instead, use time with you as the primary incentive. However, if you occasionally give your child a special dessert or treat, you may want to incorporate this already-established tradition into your reward system.

Use your reward system as a jump-start. Because the novelty will wear off quickly, update and revise the rewards often.

3. *As you have success with one positive behavior, add another.* To your child, being in control at mealtime is a very different notion from being in control when a friend won't share. Add one small step at a time.

4. *With each new step, role-play several options your child may use in the situation.* You may want to give him at least three simple strategies to be in control. For example, if another child won't share, you can help your child think of three choices for what to do: (a) He may wait and ask again; (b) he may play with another toy; or (c) he may ask a grown-up for help.

5. *Show interest and enthusiasm for all of the choices your child suggests to be in control.* You might set up a chart system to keep track of his choices and his responses during difficult situations.

6. *Remember, the time and attention you spend with your child, discussing and anticipating positive behavior, is even more important than the rewards you have promised.* Your goal is to fade out material rewards and establish yourself and your time together as the main motivators.

Behavioral Contracts and Guidelines

The older child must be a key part of any contract system you develop to set goals for change. (See Chapter 20 for information on how to use contracts as part of a family problem-solving plan.) From the beginning, your child needs to help define the anger problem and its positive replacement, the "in-control" goal. Your child also should discuss the behaviors that *you* need to change and help make a contract for your goal as well.

Make your definitions of goals as specific as possible; "being in control" is too vague. *Make clear what, when, where, and how long the new behavior must occur. Then write it down!*

Some children will respond well if their contract includes daily points, which they can trade for daily privileges and activities or save for special events that cost more points. Some teens and preteens work hard for cash incentives. Others are much more motivated by phone privileges, TV time, friends over for pizza or sleepovers, ski days or other incentives.

Following is an example of how one family successfully used a behavioral contract.

Twelve-year-old Beth had always been strong-willed, but now she seemed angry all the time. Her parents had no idea what was causing her storms. Raging hormones, disappointments with friends, frustrations at school? Who could tell? Even a simple "Good morning" triggered a yelling match. If her parents told her they wanted her to go out to dinner with them, Beth would scream that she never had any time with her friends. If they told her she could go to her friend's house only after she had cleaned the bathroom, Beth would hurl the cleaning supplies onto the floor.

Bewildered and overwhelmed by the intensity of their daughter's rage, her parents tried everything to subdue her: ignoring her tantrums, lecturing her, and imposing harsh punishments that were impossible to enforce. If they grounded her for two weeks, they would inevitably lift the restriction after two days of Beth's whining and pleading. What to do?

Beth's family called a family summit to try to resolve the conflict. First, they drew their family's Rage Gauge. Each member was asked to identify three changes they could make in themselves and three changes each of the other members could make to improve family life. When Beth complained that her parents were too bossy and strict, they asked her to restate her wishes in the form of positive things they could do in specific situations.

Beth said she wanted to be in control of herself; she did not want any reminders from her parents about doing her chores. They agreed to make a chore list and to let Beth keep her own schedule, as long as she completed all of her chores by Saturday at noon. If she did, she would have free access to her friends the next week.

Her parents asked Beth to speak with them in a quiet, respectful tone of voice. Beth countered that they should *all* do this. The family agreed that if any member spoke in a belligerent or nagging tone, he or she would have to do three chores on the other's list. The family completed their contract by putting it in writing.

Once her parents had made an equal commitment to changing their behavior, Beth felt empowered and acted more mature. She delighted in catching her mom and dad in angry tirades. It took her parents several times of having to do Beth's chores before they were able to break the bad habit of nagging. (They had seen their fussing as "helpful reminders.")

Her parents finally recognized that their lectures had helped to trigger Beth's tantrums. By setting a contract that focused on both sides of the conflict, child *and* parents, this family succeeded in establishing effective anger control.

It didn't happen overnight, however. After the first week, Beth was still sighing and slamming things down, although her tone of voice had improved. At the family meeting to review the contract after a week, Beth's parents said she could have phone privileges each day only if her body language, as well as her voice, was respectful. (They could easily enforce this restriction by unplugging the phone and taking it to work.) Only one day of this ban was necessary. Social time to talk to friends was so important that Beth was motivated to be in control.

Without the constant hassles, her family had more time for listening to Beth and began to understand many of the pressures she faced as a young adolescent. Having her parents as a sounding board helped her reduce tension. She was able to identify sources of anger with peers and teachers. In the safe haven of her family, she could think of and evaluate possible solutions to her conflicts before risking the rejection of her friends.

The preceding example illustrates the following key issues in developing a contract to deal with angry older children:

1. *Be democratic.* Identify the problem as the entire family's responsibility. This will reduce defensiveness and will create a climate of cooperation and mutual responsibility for solutions.

2. *Be positive.* Set clear, well-defined expectations for change. Anticipate typical scenarios. Use these to define what is expected when.

3. *Let your child define what she will do to be in control.* Be open and flexible to your child's perspective. Does it really matter when the bed is made or the homework is done, as long as your teen is responsible?

4. *Use social activities as rewards for appropriate behaviors.* These are immensely powerful motivators for teenagers.

5. *Anticipate a positive response.* Praise positive behavior when you see it.

6. *Ask for help when you are having difficulty maintaining control.* Let your child be a consultant to you. Show her that parents are human. Ask for her suggestions about how *you* can be in control and how this will help. We all feel angry, we all make mistakes, and we all need the help and support of others.

7. *Expect everyone to blow it sometimes.* Be low-key in your reac-

tion. Include in your plan how everyone will remain calm and how other family members can be most helpful to the one who is out of control.

8. *Set firm consequences for misbehavior.* Violations must be fined. Loss of social privileges or extra work detail are the most effective strategies. Use only the consequences that you can fully enforce. For example, if you remove TV time, does the rest of the family lose theirs as well? Will your teenager sneak phone time before you come home from work? Unless you lock up the phone or TV, these consequences may not work. Brief restrictions are much easier to monitor and, in the long run, more effective. Extra work detail can give you a sense of being "paid back" for your teen's rampage. Working to pay off the person she injured or insulted can teach her a sense of accountability, empathy, and responsibility.

Punishment as Discipline

Although punishment is the disciplinary method most parents think of first, it should be used *sparingly*. Parents tend to punish when their own and their children's anger is white-hot. In this emotional climate, the potential for further conflict is high. If you must use punishment, try to use it early in the angry buildup—and *always* give a warning! Tell your child that if he does not begin performing an appropriate behavior within a specified time, the punishment will follow. *Never* be out of control when you set a punishment. Wait until you are calm to decide which consequences are called for.

The following are discussions of the most effective types of punishment: Positive Practice, Time-Out, Restrictions and Fines, and Restitution.

The "Positive Practice" Strategy

Positive practice is a punishment strategy, yet it requires your child to practice being in control: *After an angry outburst, your child must practice the appropriate skill and practice it many times until it is boring and "overlearned."*

Keep the practice simple and repetitive. For example, if your son slams the door each time you ask him to take out the garbage, you can require him to go out the door twenty times, shutting it as softly as possible. If your daughter screams at you if she wants you while you're using the phone, she can practice whispering "Excuse me" and writing a note to you about what she needs.

If your teen stomps around and complains each time it's his turn to do the laundry, you can require him to go into each room of the house three times, pick up and put all dirty clothes into the washer or basket, and politely ask family members if they need more laundry done.

Positive practice works best when your child needs help remembering to replace an *inappropriate action* with a *positive action*. Your child should do the practice as soon as possible after the misbehavior. If your child resists the positive practice, you should give a warning signal. By the count of ten after the signal, your child should be performing the positive practice. If so, praise your child; if not, a previously agreed-on punishment should follow.

Time-Out

Standing in the corner, going to their rooms, and sitting quietly for a specified period are all time-tested ways of helping children control their anger. Time-outs are effective because they separate angry people and provide for physical relaxation and a calming time for thinking about the problem.

If your child has trouble with tantrums and angry outbursts, a time-out can be very effective as your first choice. You can use other discipline strategies later if the time-out does not bring the problem under control.

Here's how to use time-out to calm your child's Dragon:

1. As with any punishment, be sure to warn your child before beginning the time-out. Say calmly, "If you don't calm down and do [the expected positive behavior], you will take a time-out." Then no more discussion! No bargaining after the warning.

2. Set one minute of time-out for each year of your child's age.

3. Ignore all comments and yelling while your child is in time-out. If he leaves the time-out spot, take him back with no comments, and start the time over for leaving the spot or for being aggressive.

4. If, at the end of the agreed time-out, your child is still out of control, let him know the time has ended and that he can come out as soon as he is completely calm. (A buzzer is more effective than your voice.)

5. When he is calm, ask if he is ready to come out, to be calm and to do the expected positive behavior.

6. If he says "Yes," immediately praise even his smallest steps toward positive action.

7. If he resists, says "No," or makes no comment, then the time-out starts again.

8. Do not provide much discussion at this point. Your child should be emphatic in his "Yes" before he can leave time-out.

Many parents wonder whether it is appropriate to hold a squirming, kicking child in the time-out corner. The answer is *no!* Your presence provides attention. Restraint will likely make your child angrier and more out of control. Use another strategy, such as restrictions or restitutions (discussed later in this chapter) as a back-up consequence for time-out.

Some difficult children truly have a hard time calming and consoling themselves. These overwhelmed, sensitive, intense children need strategies to get in control. They need extra help with calming the rage within (see Chapter 17). Chapter 25 will give you extra help to console, understand, and discipline an anxious, high-strung child.

What if your child trashes the room when sent to time-out? The first time, make her clean up and repair all damage. The second time, do the same, plus impose a hefty fine or loss of privilege. Thereafter, change the location of the time-out. Very active, aggressive children do better with a time-out spot that is indestructible. You can outfit a small room or part of a hall for time-out by providing a beanbag chair or pillows and quieting activities such as tapes, Legos, books, or magazines.

Is physical restraint ever appropriate? Only in rare instances. If your child is clearly endangering himself or others, and no other intervention has worked, then you must use restraint to prevent injury.

Touching your child will likely make him more agitated, so you must be strong enough to take control. Take your child firmly by the arms and hold them to his side. Say, "You need to get in control." Say nothing else.

Be an example by speaking calmly, acting relaxed, and taking several deep breaths. If your child is not under control after one minute, say, "I am going to start counting. For each number I count, you lose [number of minutes] of [a special privilege or favorite activity.]" When your child has stopped resisting physically, let go. Begin the time-out immediately.

Restrictions and Fines

Think of the many times you have said, "If you don't clean your room, you can't go to your friend's house." Or "If you keep up that tantrum, no TV for a week." Or "If you take your brother's toy one more time, I'm taking it away from both of you." Or "If you don't stop yelling at me, you can't go to the movie tonight."

Restrictions and fines are the most common form of punishment. To be effective, the penalties should include these guidelines:

1. *Deliver as promised.* Threats, unless they are authentic, not only get you nowhere but can actually increase the intensity and frequency of your child's misbehavior.

2. *Make the restriction or fine something important to your child.* For younger children, try loss of toys, food treats, special games or activities. For older children, try loss of time with friends, or restriction from video games or television. For teens, try restriction from friends; removal of phone, TV, or car privileges; or restriction from social events.

3. Never *take away a privilege your child has already earned as a reward for positive behavior or as a part of a behavioral contract.*

4. *Give your child advance warning about the nature of the restriction* *or fine.* Use your family's special "signal" or give a final warning before imposing the penalty. You must be calm and in control before imposing the fine.

5. *With older children, discuss and negotiate possible fines or restrictions in advance.* Keep a list in writing of possible penalties, even if they are not part of a formal behavioral contract. If you can point to the written agreement, you have removed the opportunity for manipulative discussions along the lines of "You never told me that," "That's not fair," or "That's not what you said. You said . . ."

6. *As with any punishment method, use restrictions and fines sparingly.* In your plan, always give your child the opportunity for getting back in control before you impose a penalty. Avoid taking away an activity that is important to your child's self-esteem or that is an effective, calming tension-reducer.

Restitution

When your child has deeply hurt or injured someone, restitution is the most effective form of discipline. Victims should be compensated for their losses. Your child should make a formal apology as the first phase. An older child can ask the victim what to do to undo the hurt, and he or she can suggest several ideas. The victim must always approve of whatever is to be done. Restitution is most effective when your child has been in aggressive conflict with other children.

Restitution does not have to be elaborate. You can easily establish a restitution system at home. When the conflict is between siblings, do not consider or discuss "who started it." If both children are misbehaving, mutual restitution is in order. The restitution should be an action that actually makes life easier for the wronged party, such as doing chores for a set time, reading a story to a younger sibling, repairing a bike, sacrificing TV choice, or giving up video-game time to the other person.

Restitution is also appropriate when *you* are the target of your child's angry outbursts. Be reasonable in what you expect. Do away with any "slave mentality." Try to make the restitution fit the violation. For example, if your teen has thrown a fit because you have to use the car tonight and she cannot use it, use a wash-and-wax job as restitution. If your six-year-old has just tossed his green beans across the room because you said he had to eat all his vegetables, make him clean them up and mop the floor for you, as well. If your ten-year-old has a tantrum over emptying the garbage, make her scrub the trash cans.

Remember to be constructive in how you use restitution. Do not frame it as a punishment. Instead, use it as an extension of an apology and a way to right a wrong. Restitution is the opportunity for renewed trust and the starting point for more appropriate decisions next time.

Calm the Dragon within You
before You Discipline

When the Dragon of Anger roars inside you, it is natural to feel out of control. You are in a state of crisis. Your anger builds to a sense of urgency and a need for release. It's crucial to *delay decisions about discipline until you are calm.* Speak to your child in a calm voice or not at all. Don't be afraid to say, "I need a break. Let's talk again in fifteen minutes."

Here are some ideas to help you calm down:

1. *Take a preventative approach.* Make a list of consequences for those nonnegotiable, absolute rules. Decide in advance what you will do when your child hits, curses, comes home late, lies, and so on. Let your child help decide the disciplinary consequences. Write them down and post the list. When these nonnegotiable rules are broken, you are ready. Stay quiet. Stay calm. Follow through!

2. *Pay close attention to your internal "rage gauge" during these volatile times.* Your anger may cause you to overreact. You may misread and distort information because of your own intense emotions. If your "feeling" temperature is getting high, it is essential that you get under control.

3. *Use your cool-down strategies. If they don't work, take a time-out.*

4. *Do not repeat your position; this only enrages your child.* We often become stubborn and self-centered in the heat of anger. We believe our position is right.

5. *Take time to take perspective.* Let your child know that you both are having trouble hearing and understanding each other when you're angry. Say, "When we're both calm, I'll be more able to talk and understand your point of view."

By opening the door to understanding, you are not necessarily agreeing. You are setting the stage for important connections. Communication is a key to Taming the Dragon.

Few crises are as difficult as they seem at first. Get in control and find a way to be calm. When you are in control of yourself, you will be much better able to decide on an effective discipline plan for your child.

Your improved communication with your child and newly acquired discipline techniques will be an important advantage as you read the next chapter and discover suggestions for helping your child learn to resolve conflicts with other kids.

23

Dragon against Dragon

CONFLICTS WITH OTHER KIDS

As your children grow, you may worry about whether they will be able to cope out there in the real world, during the inevitable angry storms of childhood and adolescence. You cannot always be there, of course (and your children would not want you to fight their battles), but there is much you can do to help them handle their feelings.

Throughout this book you have been learning to understand your children's development and to match your strategies to their ages and stages. In this chapter, you will learn to help your children deal successfully with teasing, bullying, and peer pressure. You will find suggestions for letting your children manage their own problem solving and develop the confidence to risk failure with their own solutions.

Preschoolers' Conflicts: Territory and Possessions

Preschoolers are striving for control of their own bodies; they also want to be "Master of the Universe." Their focus is still limited to "Me, me, me!" The subtleties of asking and bargaining are often beyond them. They would rather grab and take.

Typical conflicts at this stage center on territory and possessions. "This is mine!" "My dog is better than yours." "You can't have it!" If they cannot get their way, preschoolers may threaten, "I just won't be your friend any more if you don't do it my way." A more sophisticated and polite child may polish the threat to, "If you give me it, I'll still be your friend." The intent is the same, however—to get their own way.

Teach Your Preschooler to Take Turns

Blowups run high at this stage. Pushing, grabbing, throwing, and hitting are common expressions of anger. Parents send their little ones to preschool so they can learn "social skills," then wonder why they have so much trouble handling their child at home when only one playmate comes over!

> *Jeremy was the original knight in shining armor, staking out his territory and conquering dangers. With his baby brother, he developed elaborate fantasies of rescues so that Jeremy could be strong and in control. When friends came over to play, he insisted that they play his way. Jeremy knew he should "take turns" and let the others boys be the hero, but he couldn't resist telling the other knights exactly what to do.*
>
> *His bossiness soon led to shouting and pushing. His father warned, "If you can't play nicely, your friend is going home." Jeremy screamed and hurled the knight's plastic sword at his friend, shouting, "He started it! It's all his fault!"*

If Jeremy's father sent the friend home, what would Jeremy learn? How could Dad help each child learn something from this? Did the boys need to focus on their feelings or on what to do to solve the problem?

Preschoolers cannot yet talk through their problems. They will only get frustrated if a parent tries to get them to negotiate a compromise. Jeremy's dad decided to help the boys *define their territories* and to be clear about what taking a turn would mean:

> *"I know each of you likes to have a turn being knight," Dad said, "and I am proud of you for sharing. Sometimes we all want to tell the other guy how to take his turn. This only makes everybody mad. When you take a turn, you get to be completely in charge of what the knight gets to do. If the dragon doesn't like it, he will have to wait until his turn to change things. How can we help the dragon be patient and wait his turn?"*

This technique avoids having the parent take over, and lets the preschoolers have one well-defined area of control. Defining territory made clear what was Jeremy's and what was his friend's. Dad helped the children focus on what they would need to do to cope. He also was clear about what issue they needed to handle: learning to wait calmly until it was their turn to be in control.

> *When the boys returned to their game, Dad kept a watchful eye. He praised the dragon for the various creative ways he challenged the*

*knight and waited for his turn. He noted with pride how each had
staked out his own territory and was able to share. He was prepared
to respond with time-outs if either child got out of control.*

Tips to Help Your Preschooler Get Along

Remember these points when helping your preschooler handle conflicts
with other children:

1. *Actions speak louder than words.* If you want your child to learn
to share calmly and negotiate, you must be a good example. Do not yell
and threaten. Be a good model for what you are hoping to see in your
child.

2. *Clearly define the territory.* Accept that preschoolers need to have
"mine and yours." If they can't be clear about whose is whose, help them
do it. Praise them for what they have worked out as turns or possessions.
Help them clarify who gets what, then let them work out that goal and
try it.

3. *Help your child use words and not actions.* Children of this age
often try to "speak" through their actions. Grabbing often comes before
the "Can I have that toy for a while?". Pretend that you are a movie
director, and push the "pause" and "rewind" buttons. Replay which
words helped to promote sharing and decrease anger. "Erase" the physical outbursts by being clear that "grabbing and hitting are not allowed."
Ask what would have been a better way to use words to ask for what you
want.

4. *Words are tools, not weapons.* Even a four-year-old needs limits
set on yelling, cursing, and threatening. Quickly interrupt nasty tirades
by being clear that this is unacceptable. Let your child know you understand that he is mad or frustrated. Let him know that you and his friend
will not listen to shouting and name-calling. Ask him to say what he wants
in a nice way.

5. *When your child is truly out of control, it's time for discipline.*
Prolonging an angry tirade by insisting that your child talk when she is
out of control is futile. Take a deep breath and ask your child to calm
down. Go back to Step 1 when she is calm. If she is agitated, blaming
everyone else, or becoming more out of control, it's time for immediate
discipline. Time-out is most effective for this age because it gives your
child a time to think and cool down. Then you can go back to Step 1.

School-Agers' Conflicts:
Pressure from the Group

Most school-age children have enough self-control to be able to invite a
group of friends over to play without the drama of shoving matches and

shouts of "It's mine!" The gang will spend much time charting their list of rules for play. It's no accident that clubs, sports, board games, and video games are popular at this stage. They provide a format for what are acceptable ways to play and allow independence from parents but include enough structure to reduce chances for conflict.

Belonging to the group is the only goal that matters for most ten-year-olds. By conforming to the group's expectations and rules, children get a sense of security and acceptance. We parents are reassured when our children choose friends and activities whose values and rules are acceptable to us. We become worried and frightened when we sense negative influences and peer pressures that may sway our children in the wrong direction.

Rejection and Bullying

Peer conflicts at this stage often center on group acceptance. The group can be cruelly intolerant to differences of style or opinion and will reject any child who disagrees or seems in any way odd or nonconformist. Kids therefore learn to mask their feelings. Instead, they act out their anger in indirect ways, perhaps at their parents, or maybe ridiculing, teasing, or playing humiliating practical jokes on another child, to wound as they have been wounded.

At the other extreme are the bullies who use power and intimidation to enforce their view of the way things should be. Bullies may be masking a feeling of powerlessness or using control and revenge tactics that they have learned at home. Whatever the reasons, we parents often feel frustrated as we try to help our children cope with a bully's actions. Even more difficult is knowing what to do when our own child becomes the bully.

> Travis had always been a careful boy, shy and hesitant about making friends. He was never chosen for any group activities and often felt left out. When he joined the school swim team and found success, his parents were relieved and delighted. Travis's agility and quick stroke earned him medals in the competitive meets. If he lost, however, he became bitterly angry. So far he had managed to confine his blowups to the car or the safety of home, but the situation changed when Rod moved down the block.
>
> A championship swimmer, Rod was Travis's opposite in style: bold, brassy, and outgoing. If Rod lost a swim meet to Travis, he immediately had to come up with a way to save face. He would resort to his repertoire of taunts and destructive practical jokes (in the locker room, behind the coach's back, of course) to retaliate against Travis.
>
> With everyone laughing at him, Travis felt put down, rejected, and very angry. He began blowing up and cursing if he lost a meet,

and even threw a towel at a referee. When Rod pulled Travis's pants down and called him a "weenie," Travis hit Rod, giving him a bloody nose. The coach called Travis's parents with serious concerns about their son's unsportsmanlike conduct.

Travis's parents felt they already had tried everything to help him handle Rod's bullying. They had told Travis to "just ignore it" and "keep your cool." Travis had refused to let his parents confront Rod about his outrageous behavior, for fear of more embarrassment and ridicule. In fact, Travis had been hiding many of the incidents that angered him because he was afraid his parents would take action. Travis also knew that going to the coach for help would mark him as a "wimp" and a "tattletale."

Travis's parents went to the coach and to another boy on the team for more information. Both had urged Travis to "lighten up and chill out," because his quick temper made him an easy mark. The friend revealed many of the details of Rod's baiting and taunting, after a promise that the parents would not reveal his involvement. (The boy did not want to become Rod's next target.)

The parents then told the coach what they had learned and how stuck they felt at not being able to control Rod's behavior, which they saw as a trigger to their son's rages. The coach agreed to supervise the locker room more closely and to intervene with any boy who was being unsportsmanlike. But the coach was also quite clear: *Travis would have to learn to handle this problem himself.*

Travis needed to take control and to do it in an active way. Ignoring the problem would not work. His parents could not do it for him. Yet Travis needed an ally. He needed his teammates behind him. The parents invited Travis's friend over for pizza and helped the boys come up with a *plan of action.*

Travis and his friend decided that trying to negotiate or talk things out with Rod wouldn't work, at least not yet. They agreed that Travis needed allies and a face-saving way to take control. They thought of several jokes and comebacks that illustrated that Travis could handle Rod's taunts and still remain on top and in control.

With Rod's next insult, Travis would say, "Thanks, Rod. I need some trash like this so I can practice staying cool for those jerks from the Sharks—who I'm going to cream next week in the meet." If Rod continued, Travis's friend would come in with a backup, "Gee, I guess you really want Trav to win!"

The result at first was that Rod increased his put-downs, but Travis was ready with more jokes. It was Rod who finally blew it, exploded, and had to be disciplined by the coach. Travis was secretly glad when Rod was benched from a big meet for losing his temper. Travis was especially elated because he knew that, if he hadn't changed his ways, he would have been sitting on that bench instead!

Tips to Help School-Age Kids Help Themselves

The previous example illustrates several key points to keep in mind when you are trying to help your child handle conflicts with peers:

1. *Always try to talk it out first.* If you are using the communication ideas from Chapter 19, prompt your child to try them, too. Kids, as well as parents, can effectively use "I statements," which clarify feelings and state what you want, rather than what you don't want.

2. *Help your child plan ways to solve problems, negotiate, and compromise.* If the other child is responsible and reasonable and wants to be friends, these techniques will usually work. Be an adviser and help your child figure out what went well, then come up with ideas for how to talk even better the next time.

3. *Help your child cope and feel in control.* Keeping a positive self-image is essential for school-age children to feel that they belong and are accepted. Emphasize that mature, popular kids keep their cool. Using her sense of humor, developing special skills at which she excels, or joining another friend all demonstrate that "I can handle this." Help your child gain control and confidence by practicing the relaxation and calming strategies discussed in Chapter 17.

4. *Avoid taking over.* School-age children have a strong need to be capable and to be accepted by the group. The last thing a ten-year-old wants is for Dad to step in. How embarrassing. If discipline is needed outside the home, let the teachers, coaches, friend's parents, or other supervising adults be the ones to intervene publicly.

You might privately meet with these adults and steer them toward discipline that emphasizes restitution, making amends, and developing rules to prevent further blowups. Enlist your child's friends as allies only if you can do so by keeping your child actively involved and in control.

5. *Discipline if your child can't get under control.* Even after you have tried other appropriate ways to help your child solve the problem, he may still be raging. To let him stay out of control only puts him at further risk of being ridiculed, rejected, or punished by teachers or coaches. It is time to step in and remove some privileges, especially those that are directly involved in his current problem.

He also should make restitution to those whose feelings have been hurt by his flare-ups. Make good use of the time your child spends being grounded or in time-out. Make him responsible for developing his own cool-down and be-in-control plan.

Teens' Conflicts: Too Many Changes

The world of friends and peers becomes even more vital when your child reaches the teen years. With your teen's growing independence, you will abdicate even more control—and rightly so. Your teen will continue needing to belong and to be accepted. However, with a growing need for independence also comes a need to be different and individual. Most teens are caught in a push-pull dilemma: *"I want my friends to accept and like me, but I also want to be my own person—special, unique."*

Teens clearly mark their "in" groups and "out" groups with names and territories, so that they can rebel and be different but still keep allies during their experiments with nonconformity. The rules for group behavior shift rapidly, as do the alliances within groups. A friend one day may be an enemy the next.

Finding a balance between sameness and difference, and intimacy and separateness, is a tough challenge. This ambivalence also is apparent in many teens' dating patterns. They want to be close, but they are also terrified of rejection. They may use anger to push a "steady" away when the relationship becomes too close, or too hot, to handle.

Handling a Headstrong Teen

Competition for status and esteem is exciting and frustrating. Teens want to be considered "the best" at something and are especially sensitive to a loss of face within the group. Loss of status often triggers anger and rage, which may mask the hidden hurt and fear of failure.

> *Stormy had been true to her name since she was a little girl. Never very talkative, she was sensitive and quick to anger. As a toddler, she would lash out with throwing and hitting if things did not go her way. Her parents were verbal, analytical people who could not understand why their daughter's style was so opposite from their own.*
>
> *Over the years, they had learned to help Stormy use physical exercise and sports to get control of her anger. They felt she was making real progress—until her first year of high school, when Stormy became increasingly out of control.*
>
> *At home she was grumpy, belligerent, and generally on strike, refusing to do her chores. She tested the limits of any adult-imposed rules and stopped trying at school, truly believing that this school year did not count. She was sure that no college admissions office would look at her ninth grade transcripts. Her parents were most concerned*

at how isolated Stormy had become socially. After bouncing from group to group, she withdrew, rather than risk further rejection.

Now Stormy had fallen in love. Her relationship with her boyfriend was characteristically intense. One day they would be passionately together, then would have a bitter fight and break up, only to kiss and make up the next day. Her parents wondered, "How much of this is normal?" Soon Stormy's fights with her boyfriend became more violent. The cursing, pushing, and slapping seemed downright abusive, and it was Stormy who was the abuser. She was on the verge of losing her boyfriend—her last friend and emotional anchor.

Parents of headstrong teens face a universal dilemma: What should you do when your teen is in conflict—and when and how far should you step in? Confrontation just tends to increase everyone's anger. Lectures only make your teen feel more guilty.

Stormy's parents were afraid to make her stop seeing her boyfriend; they knew she needed some emotional connection. They also predicted that their headstrong daughter would run away or sneak out to see him if they restricted her access to him. They liked the boy, but didn't know how to approach him about the problem. How could they give Stormy the support and guidance she needed to regain control of her life and enjoy her relationships?

First, her parents went to the school counselor for perspective on how others saw Stormy: as a capable, feisty girl who could excel at sports or drama, where her intensity and physical style would be valued. Everyone was concerned about Stormy's withdrawal and her touchiness. The counselor thought that she had isolated herself and suggested that Stormy's former friends would give her another chance if she reached out and tried to reconnect. Fortunately, she had not been explosive to teachers. The counselor was concerned about her arguments with her boyfriend during lunch hours, but the school would not intervene.

Stormy's parents decided to become good examples for their daughter. Dad began talking about how he had been so busy at work that he had not had time to call his friends or to exercise. He asked Stormy's help in making a plan to get him going. Mom remembered the anxieties she had felt during her early dating. She had slapped several boys for indiscretions. She shared memories with Stormy of her confused feelings about being close and about sexuality. She laughed about the mistakes she had made.

When the family watched TV shows or heard a song that illustrated the pangs of love, Stormy's parents used these as avenues to talk about "What If?" The more outrageous or old-fashioned their ideas, the more Stormy enjoyed setting them straight with some realistic ideas of her own. Finally she was talking to her parents.

Her parents started inviting Stormy's boyfriend on more family and group activities to expand the couple's circle of friends. This strategy helped the teens to lessen the intensity of their relationship while still making Stormy feel that her parents accepted her boyfriend.

Mom and Dad also set a clear list of ground rules: no temper tantrums, cursing, or physical outbursts. Regardless of who started it, everyone involved would have consequences: to weed the lawn *and* to come up with a prevention plan that the parents must approve before the teens could be together again.

Of course, Stormy would always be intense and volatile, but her parents knew that this was part of her charm. They just wanted her to change course and channel all that energy in a new direction. They insisted that she have one "passionate pursuit"—and they did not mean her boyfriend! Stormy chose community theater. There, she could risk failure outside of school, and she developed enough acting ability to join the high school drama club the next year.

Tips to Guide Your Teen toward Handling Conflict

What can you do to help your own headstrong teen? Be a leader and provide guidance. Have your "safety net" ready, but allow your teen to take some independent risks.

1. *Build on the skills and lessons you have learned at earlier stages.* You know best your child's strengths and weaknesses. Shape and mold these. Don't expect a volatile child to talk things out calmly. Offer the opportunity to talk, but also provide physical outlets to cool down and experience control and success.

2. *Talk in the third person.* Most teens find it too threatening to talk about their own fears and confusions. "I" and "me" are too close to handle. Create some emotional distance by using yourself as an example of human frailties (even if you have to stretch the truth with some creative stories). Your child will rise to the challenge of correcting her prehistoric Mom or Dad. Use examples of other teens, from your child's circle of friends, or those in the media, as examples to illustrate dilemmas. Always emphasize that your teen can think of creative, humorous, and practical ways to handle the conflicts. "How would you handle that?" is an important opener for discussions.

3. *Respect your teen's right to make decisions.* Even if you disagree with the plan, let your teen take a risk, as long as the plan respects the rights of others and is nonviolent. You can anticipate results by asking, "What if this, that, or the other happens?" Help your teen plan ahead and think through the impact of his actions. But be clear that he has the right to deal with his anger in his own way.

4. *Provide a safety net.* You must set clear boundaries. If your teen is self-destructive or violent to others, you must intervene. Administer fair discipline that provides opportunities for getting calm and making amends for mistakes. Make sure your teen has enough chances to feel unique and successful. If her school and peer group don't provide what she needs, look for other resources.

5. *Accept the storminess of adolescence.* Be realistic. Do not expect that your teen should have no conflicts with you or with peers. Keep your perspective and your sense of humor. Let your teen know that he (and you, too) will always face conflicts and that you are confident he (and you) can handle them. Everyone gets angry. You are there to help your teen develop ideas and solutions to anger problems. You can be a sounding board. Be an example by staying calm and being a good listener. Be ready to brainstorm ideas and support your teen's attempts to handle the situation.

When your teen senses your acceptance, rather than your judgment, she will come to you—although her first approaches might be challenges and attacks. Try not to be defensive. Reinforce the positives you see and hear. Send a message of acceptance: You trust that your teen can handle conflict, learn from the inevitable failures, and take pride in success.

Now that we've looked at ways to help your child cope with conflicts with other children, in the next chapter we'll explore ways for parents to teach siblings about conflict resolution.

24

Dragons at War
CONFLICTS BETWEEN
BROTHERS AND SISTERS

Fighting is not only a normal but also an *essential* part of brotherly and sisterly love. Why? Children need a practice ground to rehearse their skills at making friends and enemies. All kids need a time when they don't have to be good or in control; they trust the family will love them, no matter what.

Power and control are exciting and are easy to establish for the bigger and older child. Competition for status, for possessions, for time and, especially, for attention will spur your children to fight. Most of all, kids like to fight because it's *fun!* As entertainment, fighting is Number One. What excitement to provoke Brother into one of his tizzy fits! What joy to see Sister lose it, especially in front of that boy she's trying so hard to impress. What better entertainment during a long, boring car trip than to spar and duel? What quicker way to get Mom and Dad's attention? What fun just to tease, wrestle, provoke, and aggravate!

In this chapter, you will learn to recognize "normal" fighting between brothers and sisters and to know when, why, and how to step in between two raging children.

> "*I know my kids really do love each other, but why can't they ever get along?*"
>
> "*It seems like my two boys never stop fighting.*"
>
> "*I thought older sisters were supposed to be kind and helpful. My daughter spends all of her time bossing the other two, and when that doesn't work, she hits them.*"
>
> "*When do I step in? What do I do to stop this constant battle?*"

Parents want their homes to be havens of peace and security, but the tensions caused by fighting brothers and sisters can drive any parent to say, "I wish these kids had never been born!" Sometimes, in desperation and exasperation, we all find ourselves reduced to our children's level of threatening, name-calling, and intimidation. Take heart. Forgive yourself for these normal lapses. Your child certainly will forgive you.

If your goal is to eliminate your children's fighting, you will never succeed. *Think hard about whom the fighting is really bothering.* If your children seem to enjoy it and not be hurt by it, you may need to find ways to escape and relax in another part of the house. However, if the fighting is leading to physical and emotional harm, or if the same problems continually recycle and never get resolved, then you need to take action.

"But She Started It!"

The following example is a typical scenario of sibling conflict.

> *Reagan never took responsibility for her part in a fight. Not only was she too proud and stubborn to admit she was wrong, she also was a master at calling in a parent when things were not going her way and her brother was out of control.*
>
> *Round #3569 happened after Reagan had been hogging the remote control during her brother's favorite TV show. Furious at her attempts to change the channel, he finally grabbed the remote control and hit her over the head. Reagan screamed, "Mom! Bobby's hitting me again! He won't let me even exist!" Bobby retaliated, "But Mom, she started it!"*

Reagan's mother was tempted to ask what had happened. She especially was interested to hear from Bobby about what Reagan had done this time to provoke the fight. She realized, however, that this would only continue the problem, because everyone would lock into their old patterns of blame. Instead, she told the two, "I know you called me in because you were feeling out of control. I am confident you can get back in control and solve this yourselves. Each of you tell me what you can do to calm down and solve this problem."

Both kids tried to lure Mom back into the old patterns with "I was just minding my own business and he/she started it!" Each time, Mom said, "But how are you going to handle it?"

Keep the following suggestions in mind when considering your plan of action to address a scene like the preceding example.

1. *Don't ever allow yourself to be drawn into a fight.* Never set yourself up to take sides. By trying to understand what happened, we often

hear only a litany of complaints about what the other one did that was all her fault. Even when you try to referee, your children will try to sway you to see their side, hoping you will gang up with them to "get" the other.

2. *Be do be clear that, when a fight has started, both children are responsible. Your job is to help them decide what to do about it.*

3. *If you want to hear about what has happened, ask each what they already have done to try to stay in control and handle the problem.*

4. *Insist that each calm down before they talk.*

5. *Focus on helping them make a plan to solve the problem now.*

Tattling

We want our children to come to us for help when they need a sounding board and resource. But often our children seek us out not when they want help, but when they're looking for power and revenge. By calling in the big guns—Mom and Dad—a child may think he will have a strategic advantage to win the fight.

> *Rick was constantly running to Dad in the evenings to report on the escapades of his brother. "Brian's being bad. He just ate all the brownies!" "D-a-a-a-d, he did it again! Brian got in my room and was messing with my baseball card collection!"*
>
> *Of course, Brian had broken another house rule, but Dad wondered why Rick was so eager to report all his brother's transgressions. What was in it for Rick if Dad jumped in, took sides and disciplined Brian? He decided there had to be more to the story.*

In wanting to be good parents and enforce the family rules, we often get deeply and innocently embroiled in our children's conflicts. If Dad disciplined Brian, Rick would likely be secretly glad that he was able to get his brother in trouble. Gloating and full of a sense of power, Rick would have won a battle in the sibling war. Brian would want to retaliate. What better way than to set Rick up by tattling to Dad and continuing the never-ending cycle?

Rick and Brian's Dad was upset that Brian had eaten the brownies. (After all, Dad had been saving up for one after dinner.) But Dad stopped himself from jumping in to referee, because he knew that rescuing Rick would give Rick a "revenge point" against Brian.

Instead, Dad said, "Gee, I bet we were both hoping for some more brownies. Rick, you take care of your disappointment. I'll take care of mine." Then later, when Dad went into the kitchen, he "discovered" that the brownies were gone and took his own action with Brian.

Brian had to pay back the family for being so greedy: He could choose to do a chore from everyone's list to make amends, or he could take his hard-earned allowance and buy a family treat to serve cheerfully.

Keep the following in mind as you strive to stop the tattling in your family.

1. *Don't encourage tattling from your children.* Tattling is often a setup for power and revenge tactics. You are the parent and should be the supervisor and enforcer of the family rules.

2. *Do encourage your children to come to you for legitimate help with problems.* Ask, "What is the problem? How have you already tried to handle it, and what can I do to help?"

3. *When the inevitable tattletale comes,* say, "I am the parent, and I am in charge of helping everyone follow the rules. I will handle it."

4. *Ask your child*:
   - "What can you do right now to make sure you are following the rules?"
   - "How are you going to stay in control?"
   - "What can you do to solve the problem?"

Revenge

Angry brothers and sisters are often quite creative in their attempts to pay back the other for perceived and real wrongs. Imagine the feeling of power and perverse joy when teasing, baiting, name calling, and setups actually work!

When children are mad, they want someone else to pay. As grownups, we know the trouble with revenge. It is a never-ending circle of anger: *You get me back; I get you back.* But how do we get our children to see the destructive costs of revenge tactics? How, indeed, when these tactics are so common in our adult world?

> *Jill took great delight in stirring up trouble. As the middle child, she had become quite skillful at getting her brothers to explode. She squealed with joy when her parents disciplined them for their outbursts. She knew that when she called her brother a baby, or threatened to tell his friends that he still wet the bed, she could get him to blow up. All she had to do to "get" her older brother was to use one of her many ploys to embarrass him in front of his friends.*
>
> *When her brothers bullied or hit her to get their own revenge, Jill became even more creative in her tactics. She spent many hours fantasizing what she could do to make them squirm.*

Sweet revenge. Who among us hasn't imagined throwing darts at a picture of the boss? Who hasn't wanted to ruin a spouse's free afternoon with a list of chores, because that's what our dearly beloved did to us last weekend? Who hasn't wanted to retaliate against a wrong? Here's how Jill's family helped her learn more productive ways to manage her conflicts.

Jill's parents had not been aware of her numerous and successful attempts to get her brothers in trouble. When Mom and Dad started setting up Jill as an example of goodness to her brothers, the boys rebeled. They started giving her a dose of her own medicine, and the revenge battles escalated into war. Once the conflict exploded, the parents realized that everyone was contributing to the buildup.

> The parents called a family meeting and talked about the many times they had fantasized about getting revenge on others. They explained the real costs of revenge and role-played the revenge cycle they were seeing in their kids. They made it clear that they would set consequences for any further revenge ploys. Then they asked the kids what they really wanted when they felt angry.
>
> Jill gradually began to talk about how left out and jealous she felt. At first her words were more revenge attacks—"You never do this. You always do that"—but she eventually responded to her parents' questions. "If you tell us what you need, we can help you feel better."

Jill needed more control and recognition in the family. Her parents decided that she could be in charge of the pets, a role her brothers had coveted. She could keep the job as long as she handled her anger responsibly. If revenge and conflict brewed, the agreed-upon discipline plan would follow.

If Jill was angry at a brother, she was to talk it out and try to reach a compromise. If she treated others fairly and as equals, they would start to treat her with more respect.

As adults, we know the difference between fantasy and reality. We know the cost of revenge. We can appreciate the fantasy as a way to think through our anger, get it out, and move on to constructive solutions. Kids, however, often get so stuck on the anger that they can't recognize the costs of revenge. They need our help to try another way.

1. *Don't minimize your child's anger.* Revenge not only is an outlet for anger, but a way to establish power.

2. *Do insist that your child handle the anger more constructively.* Use the techniques for talking about feelings and problem solving outlined in Chapters 19 and 20.

3. *Look for ways to help your child regain the power and control that revenge brings, but in a more constructive way.* Ask your child, "What will really make you feel better here?"

4. *Remember that all children want to save face and maintain a position of power.* You can help your child best by bringing everyone to a position of equality and fairness, rather than encouraging your child to put someone else down.

"But It's Not Fair!"

By far the most seductive ploy children can use in their fights is to cry out, "But you're not being fair!" Good parents strive to be equal and fair—but being fair does not mean that things have to be the same for each child. All children have different needs and styles. You are being fair when you do what is appropriate and what matches each child's needs.

> *Keith and Mitch were very close in age, and their parents often treated them as twins. From early on, if the parents did not give them each the same treatment, one or the other boy would protest, "You're not being fair." When the boys expressed their anger, they had very different styles. Keith was a physical, easily aroused boy who exploded easily. Mitch was more thoughtful and calm but could be slyly calculating in his attempts to tattle and get revenge.*
>
> *Their pediatrician recommended that the parents use time-outs for both boys' angry outbursts. The result was that Keith always seemed to be in time-out, complaining, "But Mitch started it! You're not being fair." Time-out did help Keith calm down and get back in control, but it only seemed to give Mitch more time to plan his next revenge tactic.*

Each brother in the preceding example had different ways of expressing anger, and each needed different discipline. In a family meeting, the parents explained that they were in charge of deciding what was fair. They would not listen to any more complaints about fairness.

Keith would continue to have time-out and other ways to calm down. Mitch would have to make restitution if he resorted to revenge tactics. Because he did not like having to do Keith's chores to make amends, Mitch soon stopped his revenge tactics. Things were no longer equal, but they seemed much more fair.

Use the following tips when dealing with fairness issues.

1. *Don't become a prisoner of your children's demands for fairness.* Be clear that you are in charge of deciding what each child needs.

2. *Do seek a balance.* Be confident that you provide each child enough love, support, and attention.

3. *Do not let your children prey on your guilt.* Be more confident in how you respond to each child.

4. *Remind your children that being fair does not always mean being equal.* Being fair means that each member of the family gets what they need.

What Each Child Needs

Every child needs a sense of dignity and competency. Children see these needs more literally: They want the control to do their own thing. Too often, others infringe on these rights, which leads to frustration and anger. Whenever your child is having a wave of conflicts with friends or brothers and sisters, be sure your child's basic needs are being met. This is the most important thing you can do to prevent angry battles.

The Need to be Separate

Space. Privacy. Individuality. How is your house structured? Does each child have a place to be alone, to be creative, to be quiet and calm? Can each child have friends over into a space that is theirs? Does your schedule allow private time for each family member? Does each child get separate and protected time alone with each parent?

Many battles are simply turf squabbles. By examining your household structure, your calendar, and your expectations, you can give each family member the space and separateness he or she needs. Don't forget yourself in this. If you can get the time you need for renewal and privacy, you will be more able to respond to your children's needs. You also will be able to take their normal fighting with a sense of humor and acceptance.

The Need to Feel Special

All of us need to feel special and to feel pride in our accomplishments. We need to feel in control of ourselves. Children who are most angry often feel out of control. They feel no one looks up to them. They feel powerless. They can quickly establish a sense of power and control by starting a fight. Fighting puts them on center stage. Even if they don't win or get their way, they have been the focus of everyone's attention for a little while.

If you have "tried everything" and your child is still fighting and even seems to like it, you know that the payoff must be great. Your child may not be getting enough recognition or sense of accomplishment. Try to develop activities in which your child can be unique and successful. Try to help your child value successes. You can speak with pride and brag about your child's strengths. Help your child feel special and in control of something other than the Dragon of Anger.

The Need to be Stimulated

Fighting can not only relieve tension, but boredom, too. Fighting can become a habit as addictive as television or video games. You may want to explore some new hobbies and activities to challenge and stimulate your children and their friends. For those long car trips or other boring times, you will need attractive options for creative energy, as well as clear fines for misbehavior.

What Is Your Example?

As you have learned throughout this book, *you* are an important key to helping your child Tame the Dragon. If your children are having ongoing problems with each other, you may need to take a more serious look at yourself.

How do you, as parents, handle your marital conflicts? If you are divorced, how do you and your ex manage your differences? How do you deal with your anger toward friends, relatives, and coworkers? What examples are you providing? You may need to do some long-term planning about how you will improve your relationships with others.

By thinking through what makes you angry and the implications of your choices for handling anger, you can help siblings practice learning to make better choices, too.

If your child's Dragons seem especially fiery or fierce, the next three chapters offer clues and guidance for recognizing the difference between normal behavior for children who have anxious, impulsive, or aggressive personality types and the signs that suggest when professional help may be appropriate.

PART V

SPECIAL DRAGON CHALLENGES

25

The Anxious, Highly Stressed Child

Nearly every child has flashes of explosive anger at times, without necessarily having "special needs" in anger management. However, children who are anxious and overstressed, active and highly impulsive, or aggressive and out of control present particular challenges because their rage can be so intense.

Characteristics of the Anxious, Highly Stressed Child

Characteristics of anxious, highly-stressed children may include:

- Hiding true feelings and needs
- Pushing themselves beyond their abilities
- Shying away from group activities
- Being watchful and cautious, or overly responsible and cooperative

For these children, the "straw that broke the camel's back" effect is likely. When faced with one more demand or pressure, they may suddenly become tearful, angry, and overwhelmed. Tempers may flare. Overachievers may suddenly stop trying. The resulting lowered grades or lessened success may only confirm their worst fears: that they really are hopeless failures. To defend against this fear, these children may angrily lash out, attacking and blaming others.

What Triggers Your Child's Anger?

Typical anger triggers of the anxious, overstressed child are:

- Too many pressures
- Perceived slights and criticism
- High self-expectations

Emily was an eager-to-please second-grader who had coped with a recent move, her father's remarriage, and his frequent business trips. She seemed to take everything in stride and seldom complained, but recently she had developed unusual bedtime fears and had begun an obsessive ritual when she dressed herself in the morning.

Before she would get dressed, she would first lay each piece of clothing on her bed and painstakingly smooth its wrinkles. Socks, underwear, jeans, sweater—everything had to undergo the process. If her dad or stepmother tried to hurry her or interrupt her routine, Emily exploded. Then, guilty and ashamed, she withdrew into silence and hid her emotions—until the next minor frustration, when she would blow up again.

Bright and highly verbal, anxious, overly stressed children like Emily spend a great deal of time and energy thinking and talking about themselves in unproductive, obsessive, stress-arousing, and negative ways. It is important for parents to find ways to help them turn their verbal skills into an asset. Children can learn to use "self-talk" for soothing and coping. Their own sensitivity can help them learn to interpret other people's needs, feelings, and expectations more realistically.

Ways to Help Your Overstressed Child

An anxious child will willingly take on inappropriately high levels of stress. Following are things you can do to reduce the demands on your child and remove some of the pressure. The goal for parents is to help these children feel a sense of confidence and self-worth in who they *are*, not what they *do*.

1. Praise your child for taking time to relax, go slowly, and enjoy the moment.
2. Be sensitive to your child's stress levels and try to keep your own tensions and demands in check.
3. When your child's "rage gauge" rises, provide face-saving "escape valves" that offer time to cool down and regroup.

Appropriate Discipline

Anxious children already are highly critical, masters at self-ridicule and self-recrimination. Lectures from adults only increase their guilt and anger. Punishment is seldom necessary. If we focus too much on punishment, their rage may simply move underground.

Effective discipline for highly stressed children involves time-outs and quiet projects, which give them an opportunity to calm themselves. Restitution gives them a way to reduce their guilt and overcome their fear of rejection, by joining, in a positive way, with the person whom they have hurt.

Provide Ways to Relax, Manage Time, and Establish Self-Control

Rage Gauges are often effective because they allow these children to monitor their own feelings. Their symptoms are likely to be physical signs of stress and negative self-talk. The Rage Gauge can help them recognize when to use mental and physical cool-down strategies.

Teach Positive Self-Talk. One effective technique combines physical relaxation with positive self-talk: When the child feels tension in his neck and chest, he can begin to do head rolls and slow, deep breathing. With each count of the head roll or breath out, he can tell himself, *"I can handle it. I can take it one step at a time."*

Because these children expect too much of themselves, it is important to keep the cool-down thoughts and actions extremely simple. Otherwise, they become another opportunity for obsession. Many anxious children have difficulty with these self-control exercises because their own negative, obsessive thoughts intrude, increase the pressure, and interrupt the relaxation response.

Their thoughts are generally in the form of "I should ———," "I can't ———," or "If I don't do ———, some [horrible rejection or negative consequence] will happen." Thought-stopping techniques may be necessary.

Teach Thought-Stopping. To stop the buildup of obsessive thoughts, your anxious child must first learn to identify them. Here's how to teach this effective technique:

1. *Ask your child to list obsessive thoughts on her Rage Gauge and add to the list whenever new, self-defeating thoughts replace the old ones.*

2. *Teach your child to use a signal word, as easy as "Stop!"* On this cue, she must stop the negative thoughts or statements and replace them with positive, coping statements: "I'm OK. Kids will like me more if I calm down and get in better control"; or "I can handle things better if I take the pressure off myself."

3. *Encourage your child to reward himself whenever he uses a thought-stopping technique.* (The most effective reward is the praise you give.)

Teach Self-Control. Anxious, overstressed children tend to explode into unprovoked or grossly exaggerated tirades after a long period of tension and self-blame. You may hear a litany of the wrongs you have done against your child. Be careful not to respond to this challenge, no matter how tempted you may be.

Listen closely. Underneath the attack lies an avalanche of your child's sense of failure and disappointment. Your child feels guilty and ashamed for letting you down, so he attacks you and your demands and expectations.

If a cool-down strategy does not help him to relax, cue him to use the thought-stopping technique. If he responds, praise him and negotiate a time for discussion. If he does not respond, disciplinary action (time-out, consequences, or restitution) is in order.

Reduce the Pressure. Once the floodgate has opened, your child likely will reel off a long list of grievances. Many of her complaints will be realistic and accurate assessments of the pressure under which she has been operating. Follow these steps to teach your child ways to deal with stress and conflict:

1. *Be clear that you will listen and respond once she is calm.*
2. *Start with one issue at a time.*
3. *Acknowledge your role in the problem by creating a contract for change.* As part of the contract, be sure that your child agrees to watch for her early signs of anger and pressure and, at that point, let you know what would be most helpful.
4. *Agree upon scheduled "pressure breaks."* Prevention plans are the key.
5. *Plan rewards that include more time for play, humor, and relaxation.* Help your child agree to use self-praise and positive feedback to build self-esteem.

Encourage Your Child to Talk to You

Although these children often are chatterers and intensely curious, they tend to communicate solely to gather information about what others think and need. This gives them a sense of control. However, they may mask their own needs and feelings until they reach the breaking point. You can use the following suggestions to help your child be more open about feelings. Remember, however, that getting your child to communicate is often slow and difficult. Trust and a state of calm are crucial.

1. *Initiate quiet talks about general issues, at bedtime or when riding together in the car.*

2. *Use third-person, hypothetical, or what-if situations, to give your child the needed distance for emotional issues to surface.*

3. *Discussing your own frustrations may be helpful.* Emphasize that we all have self-doubts and at times want to lash out.

4. *Do not dismiss or try to explain away the initial negative feelings that may surface when your child begins to talk.* These thoughts do not mean that he is a failure or will be rejected. It is perfectly acceptable for him to have and to share these doubts and frustrations.

5. *As he becomes more comfortable discussing feelings, let your child know you want to hear his complaints and anger toward you, as long as he expresses his views appropriately.* The sooner you hear a concern, the more easily you can respond. The more specific and positive he is, the more effective your own response will be. You can react more positively to what your child *does* want, rather than what he does not want.

When Therapy May Help

Usually the anxious, overstressed child's anger can be successfully resolved within the family. However, a crisis such as job stress, a new baby, divorce, a death in the family, or other demands may add so much tension and pressure that your family reaches a breaking point. You may be temporarily unavailable to meet your child's needs.

In these cases, family therapy is often most effective. Your child needs to see you as the key to helping restore a sense of calm. You need to be your child's support and advocate. Therapy can help your entire family share the responsibility for the problem and learn stress-reduction and coping strategies.

26

The Active, Impulsive Child

Some children are born in high gear. They act before they stop to think. Tempers flare when they can't immediately have what they want. Their frustration builds into angry tirades, which can be particularly embarrassing in public. Parents, teachers, friends, and siblings can quickly become frustrated and worn out by an impulsive child's antics.

Characteristics of the Active, Impulsive Child

Characteristics of the active, impulsive child may include:

- Social immaturity
- Difficulty playing on a team
- A seeming lack of consideration for others' feelings
- Fighting rather than talking in response to conflict
- Self-centeredness

Families with these children often find themselves emotionally drained. They may understand the need to channel their child's energy, but they cannot help feeling resentful and frustrated at times. "We've tried everything!" is their cry of surrender.

At school, the impulsive child's problems are likely to increase dramatically. She may begin a pattern of underachievement because she finds it so difficult to stay on-task. Too busy looking around at what others are doing, she may fail to complete her own assignments. Other students become irritated with her bossiness and need to be first. Her short fuse may lead to frequent minor tantrums when her teacher corrects her.

What Triggers Your Child's Anger?

Typical anger triggers of active, impulsive children are:

- Requests to be calm, controlled, and patient
- Minor frustrations, such as changes in routine or a mild increase in the difficulty of a task
- Adult-imposed limits on their impulses ("No, you can't have that candy bar; it's only an hour before dinner time.")
- Teasing, name-calling, or baiting from peers

Following is an example of the out-of-bounds behavior that is not unusual for an active child.

Eight-year-old Todd was an active boy who literally couldn't wait for anything. At the mall one Saturday with his dad and his sister Megan, he begged for ice cream. The three took their place in line at the ice cream counter, but Todd couldn't stop fidgeting. "Hurry up!" he fumed, jostling the people ahead of him. His dad told him to be polite and wait quietly, but the line was taking forever! Suddenly Todd darted ahead and tried to elbow his way to the front.

His embarrassed father took him by the arm and guided him back to the end of the line. "If you can't wait your turn politely, son, I'll have to take you out to the car to cool off, and there won't be time for us to come back and get our treat."

Todd glared, outraged, at his dad and exploded. "Great, Dad! I never get to do anything! Thanks for being so mean! I hate this family!"

Eleven-year-old Megan, who had been waiting quietly in line, turned to her brother and hissed, "Thanks a whole lot, Todd! You just wrecked another day for all of us! Maybe you hate our family, but I'm starting to hate you!"

As their exasperated father tried to hurry both children out of the mall, Megan said angrily, "It's not fair, Dad! I didn't do anything wrong, and now I don't get ice cream either—and it's all his fault!"

Todd, crying tears of rage and frustration, shouted, "Sure, Megan, sure! Everything's always my fault! You always get what you want! Sweet, innocent, dorky Megan, who never does anything wrong! Everybody knows Mom and Dad love you best!"

Their father drove home in a fog of exhaustion and bewilderment.

What should he have done to prevent this battle? How could one family produce two such completely different kids—Todd, strung high as a kite, and Megan, who seldom lost her treats or her temper? Dad felt that whatever choice he made would have been wrong. He knew he could not permit Todd to get away with his out-of-bounds behavior. But was it fair that Megan should also have to leave the mall and miss her treat?

Ways to Help Your Child Learn to Cope with Change

Establish Order, Routines, and Consistency

Order, routine, and *consistency* are vital to prevent temper outbursts. Active, impulsive children have the most difficulty coping with changes in routine. Of course, no family can develop a schedule that is carved in stone, but the more you can help your child anticipate changes, the more you can prevent the buildup of frustrations. Use the following as guidelines to help your active child:

1. *Discuss changes, new rules, and plans in advance.*
2. *If possible, let your child rehearse or role-play his responses.* (Curious and energetic, these children often make wonderful actors.)
3. *Do not try to put your child on the spot, but motivate him to be a leader or helper for the good of the group.*
4. *Teach your child how to handle waiting.* This is especially important if waiting will be part of the new or changed routine. Active, impulsive children cannot just sit and be patient. Assign an appropriate activity to pass the time, such as hanging up the coats or loading the car.
5. *Organize activities into small steps.* These children tend to rush through tasks, or get sidetracked and leave tasks only partially done. How often have you asked your impulsive child to empty the wastebaskets into the trash can, and later discovered that she has done only one room—and left the lid off the trash can?
6. *Rehearse the steps of the task.* Draw or list the steps.
7. *Encourage your child to monitor her own performance.* Have her check off what she has done.
8. *Don't jump in too soon with criticism or additional prompting (otherwise known as nagging).* If she becomes sidetracked, encourage her to monitor herself and take control.

Set Rewards and Use Incentives for Appropriate Behavior

Impulsive children are used to getting a lot of attention (even if it is negative) when they are out of control, but they are often ignored when they are *in control*. To change their behavior, you may need to use material or activity-related rewards at first. Rewards should encourage completion of each small step of a task *and* reinforce self-monitoring. Individual reward programs are very important at home. Remember that praise and attention are the most effective rewards in the long run.

> Sean often spoiled the family's outings with his overexcitement. As he waited impatiently for his family to get ready, he became rambunctious and frustrated and would hassle his brother and sister, who resented his nagging.
>
> Conflicts would build, but Sean's parents, busy with preparations, often failed to intervene at the beginning. Finally, full-blown screaming matches and hitting would bring them running to cries of "He started it!" Sean then became the center of controversy. Lectures just fueled his arguments. In time-out, he ranted and raved. His parents wondered if he could ever be in better control.

Sean's family recognized that a pattern had developed. They made a list of family rules about who was to do what to get ready for an outing. They gave Sean specific actions to perform, which kept him busy but away from his siblings. If he could complete each of his tasks (loading the car, emptying the litter bag, packing the lunches), he would earn the privilege of sitting in the front seat during the drive and distributing the gum to the other children.

His brother and sister also were given tasks and rewards related to being prompt in getting ready. (If Sean did all his tasks correctly, checked them off the list, and still had time to wait, he was instructed to go out to swing, read, or play a video game.)

Incentives and rewards should focus on the positive, self-control behaviors you want your active, impulsive child to learn. Do not expect him to be able to be patient, to sit and wait, or to talk openly and calmly about his needs and feelings. You will have more success rewarding his choice of appropriate actions to keep him occupied and to complete the expected task.

Teach Self-Control

By age eight, children can accept more responsibility for learning to stay in control. Help your child *physically practice* the following exercise (simply discussing it is not enough for active, impulsive children): "Stop, Think, Do."

How do you stop a child who is rushing off in a frenzy? How do you encourage an active child to slow down to think before she acts? The solution lies in teaching them to remember and use three simple words: *Stop* (before exploding in anger); *Think* (about getting back in control); and *Do* (what you've learned to calm down).

1. *Start by being an example.* Talk about the automatic ways you use these steps every day. Each evening, as you routinely discuss the day's incidents, include examples of how you used "Stop, Think, and Do" to your advantage.

2. *Ask your child what else you could have tried to be more in control.* Your child may particularly benefit from hearing you discuss situations in which you felt frustrated and angry but used actions and thoughts to calm yourself before talking with others about the problem.

Now you and your child are ready for *skill-building sessions*, which will prepare your child for the *Do* part of the exercise. Do not start these when your child is already upset or tired. Begin during a quiet, reflective time. First, let your child know that you are proud of how mature he is becoming and how much confidence you have in his ability to use the "Stop, Think, and Do" plan himself.

3. *Have him discuss or act out a time when he has already used these steps to stay in control.*

4. *Play "What If?", with each of you imagining frustrating situations and practicing how you could use this new skill.*

5. *Praise your child whenever you catch her using the strategy.* Keep track of the number of times she stays in control each day and reward her with an extra story or other special time with you. When she reaches an agreed-upon total during a week, she can earn a bigger reward, such as a movie-and-popcorn night.

Discipline Tools to Help Your Child with Self-Control

You may become so frustrated and exasperated with your active, impulsive child that you center your discipline on punishments, particularly those that exclude and isolate the child. Certainly, there are situations when a time-out in his room is appropriate. However, you will be more effective if you use discipline as a way to learn self-control.

Time-Outs and Physical Activity. Time-outs (if they require young, active children to sit alone) may trigger destruction and outbursts. If your child needs isolation to get under physical control, a *physical action* instead, such as walking around the yard, riding her bike around the block, or stacking wood, may be more effective. You can choose any safe activity that provides isolation and a chance to use excess energy. You can also combine time-out with restitution, by having your child do a chore for the injured party or mend a toy broken in an argument.

Positive Practice. This is a powerful disciplinary tool with impulsive children. The active child who rushes out of the house without his coat and lets the dog loose may respond with resentment and tantrums when you correct his behavior. Having him put on his coat ten times and carefully close the door twenty times may reinforce his understanding of what you expect.

You also can prompt your child to use positive practice to learn a *physical relaxation skill*. This skill is crucial, particularly for preschoolers, as a step toward mastering their bodies. Encourage your child to practice muscle tensing and releasing, such as the "rag doll" exercise discussed in Chapter 17, with deep breathing and other relaxation techniques.

Signals. Develop a signal for self-control to help your impulsive child overcome her tendency toward tantrums when she cannot get what she wants. Tell her that when she whines or has a tantrum, she will not get what she wants. Decide what the signal will be: counting to ten, singing a favorite song, or any other cue that allows some time to elapse. (Chapter 15 gives examples of signals your child can learn to use to cue herself.)

If she is calm and in control at the end of the signal, you can discuss what she wants. After you finish the signal, breathe deeply as an example for your child. Praise her if she joins you. Encourage even small attempts at self-control. If she does not regain control, then time-out or removal of privileges is in order.

Restitution. For the older child who explodes angrily with peers, restitution is especially effective. As always, prevention is best; try to establish early-warning signals and encourage him to use problem-solving strategies. However, if the conflict erupts, restitution is an important way for your impulsive child to realize how his behavior negatively affects others.

Restitution can be as simple as letting the other child go first in line, if the impulsive child has barged ahead. If his impulsive actions have cost someone else time or effort, he should ask the offended person what he can do in repayment. Adult supervision is vital during these negotiations.

Your child should not begin the restitution until he has become calm and in control. One of the purposes of restitution is to regain "face" and status within the group. This will happen only with a positive, helping spirit.

Prevention Planning. Impulsive children can also learn to use planning as a prevention strategy. Because they are not oriented to slowing down and thinking ahead, they must make an effort to think through the cause-and-effect of a situation. The Rage Gauge can be the basis of their plan. Knowing the triggers of their own and others' frustration will help them stop themselves and maintain control.

When Therapy May Help

Sometimes, despite your heroic efforts, the active, impulsive child continues to be explosive. When active children become more and more out of control, they experience rejection from peers and parents. Their self-esteem can plummet and depression may occur. An aggressive, "I don't care" attitude can mask feelings of failure and helplessness. If your child's anger is increasingly out of control, consider professional help.

Therapy can help your active child learn to control angry impulses. Newfound coping skills will rebuild a sense of competence. The desire to be in control can be satisfied, as your impulsive child takes charge of himself in positive ways. You can let go of the constant limits as your child takes charge and learns to stop and think.

27

The Aggressive, Out-of-Control Child

Even three-year-olds can become tyrants when temper tantrums turn into daily occurrences. If no one sets limits on their behavior, older children can gain complete control of their family, friends, and classrooms. Trying to reason with an overly aggressive child or encouraging her to talk about her anger may give her even more ammunition to manipulate and control others.

Characteristics of the Aggressive, Out-of-Control Child

Characteristics of aggressive, out-of-control children include:

- Physical fights with other children
- Refusal to respect classroom rules and authority
- Tendency to blame others with elaborate explanations
- Conflicts and power struggles with authority figures
- Disregard for the rights and feelings of others (swearing, cheating, stealing, disruptive behavior)

The problems of aggressive, out-of-control children may have stemmed originally from stress, impulsiveness, overactivity, abuse, or lack of training in self-control. It is often easy to excuse and overlook aggression in young children. However, by school age, their anger patterns often reach disturbing levels.

These children may relish the power and control their aggressive outbursts achieve. They may show no remorse or conscience and may not care about how their behavior affects others. In fact, they often look for another person to blame for the problem. Refusal to accept responsibility is characteristic.

This chapter will provide some answers to the following questions:

- What limits will work when adults have tried everything?
- How can bright, manipulative children satisfy their need to be in control?
- How can parents help these children find constructive ways to lead?

What Triggers Your Child's Anger?

Typical situations that trigger the anger of an aggressive child include:

- Anything that threatens to lower his sense of status and control
- Being exposed as a failure in class, on a sports team, within his family, or peer group
- Challenges to his power base—not being able to have his way, having to follow a class rule, or to complete an assignment that "bores" him

Joy was the light of her parents' life. Bright and strong-willed, she always needed to be in control. When she was three, her parents gave in to her tirades, especially at meal and bedtimes. If she refused to eat her green beans or balked at going to bed at 8 o'clock, they let her have her way. She needs more attention, they told each other. When they felt guilty for working such long hours at their careers, they let her stay up until they went to bed to keep her from whining.

When Joy entered elementary school, her parents didn't recognize how bossy and demanding she had become. They were shocked when her first grade teacher complained that Joy was lying, stealing, and even hitting other children to get what she wanted. Joy's parents blamed the teacher for being too rigid and stifling their daughter's creativity. The school staff shook their heads in disbelief at how completely Joy had her parents wrapped around her little finger.

By fifth grade, Joy had been expelled for pushing her teacher and calling her a bitch. Her parents moved her to a more permissive school for "gifted" children. By age thirteen, Joy was defying every household rule and running wild in the neighborhood. By age fourteen she had been arrested for "joy-riding" with a group of boys in a car stolen from her father's boss.

Her parents knew Joy needed limits but were afraid she would rebel even more. Joy was desperate for the safety and security limits would provide.

Your Child Needs Limits! Limits! And More Limits

Expect considerable resistance from your aggressive child. Things will get worse before they get better. If you do not set consistent limits, your child will retaliate with more tantrums and revenge tactics. Expect a difficult path.

Remember that these children need to appear strong, successful, and in control. Try to develop appropriate, face-saving options so that they can maintain a sense of status. Recognize the importance of their social networks—their friends, classmates, and teammates—and use them as sources of feedback and reward.

Establish firm boundaries and limits. You cannot allow your child to further hurt or infringe on the rights of others.

Discipline Tools to Use with the Out-of-Control Child

Develop positive incentive programs to use with the following disciplinary measures, but recognize that the positive measures will not be successful if used alone.

Time-Out

The younger aggressive child will respond to a time-out. Establish time away from the family or friends, so that she does not receive her much-needed attention. This is the child who may run from the time-out, destroy objects in the time-out room, or yell and scream for hours inconsolably. Beware! *These are diversionary tactics intended to wear you down and get you to give up.* Be prepared for this testing to intensify and to get worse when you first set limits.

If possible, have another adult ready to work with you. You may have to take your child back to the time-out several times, so be prepared to spend up to one hour in the beginning.

Time-Out Consequences. If your child remains calm and in place, he can keep his play and TV privileges for the rest of the day. Ignore all cursing and yelling from the time-out spot. The first time he leaves the time-out spot, he loses TV privileges. The next time, he loses bike time. The next time, he goes to bed one hour earlier.

Relate Fines to Important Privileges. Write them down (or draw pictures) in advance so there are no questions. As you give a time-out, simply check off which privileges she keeps or loses. When she leaves the time-out spot, count to ten. If she has not returned, she loses a privilege. *Without comment*, take her back to time-out and start the timer again. (See Chapter 22 for a more detailed discussion of time-out procedures.)

For older children, you will need to combine time-out with other methods, such as consequences and restitution. Do not expect your child to show remorse or concern for the impact of her behavior on others. However, using these standards will let her know that she will not be permitted to hurt others.

Consequences

If you can figure out what is causing your child's anger outbursts, use this as an incentive. Instead of *gaining* status, extra cookies, or playtime outside with his tantrum, your child should *lose* this treat for being out of control.

• *Use a cue, "If you aren't calm and in control by the time I count to ten, you lose any snack or treats today."* Then, no matter what follows, if your child is not behaving appropriately by the count of ten, no treat follows. Beware of manipulative attempts at bargaining. Promises to be good are not the same as being in control.

• *Establish standard consequences, instead of those that tie in directly to the current problem.* A child who loves video games, phone calls, or television will work to keep those privileges. You can develop a written plan for loss of privileges. Be sure to write them in ascending order: For the first outburst, the child loses one hour of video games; for the second, two hours; for the third, no television.

• *Combine consequences with a reward system.* Track how many anger outbursts your child typically has in one day. Agree upon a goal for improvement; for example, changing from seven to five. Set a special privilege your child can earn if the number is five, four, three, two, one, or none. Of course, the special value of the privilege should increase as the number of outbursts goes down.

Restitution

For the child with little remorse and limited conscience, restitution is an important form of discipline. As much as possible, tie the restitution to the offense. For example, if your child breaks a window, have him clean up the mess and earn the money (or withdraw money from his own savings) to pay for a new window. If your child breaks another's toy, she will replace it. If she hits another child, she will apologize and do a favor or chore for that person.

Aggressive children often display "bad attitudes"—resentment, revenge, blame, and self-justification—when required to give restitution. Simply do not discuss these diversions. For every minute that your child complains and blames, add extra requirements for restitution.

●*Emphasize that your child's choice of aggressive actions was inappropriate, regardless of what or why, and that he must right the wrong.* The other person involved may or may not choose to right his own wrongs; that is his choice and will not be a concern in your discussion or use of restitution.

●*Clear, predictable structure is essential.* Aggressive children will resent and defy limits set especially for them, because they see them as demeaning and unfair. More effective are *family* or *group expectations* for appropriate behavior and group consequences for rule infractions.

Help Your Child Gain Positive Recognition

Many aggressive children have no outlet besides anger to achieve the status and control they seek. You can help your child find productive outlets to achieve recognition and develop a sense of self-esteem. Try to find a mentor who can help your child learn a new skill. Keep trying until you find a positive way for your child to gain success and peer recognition.

Athletics is often appropriate because it provides an outlet for energy and a structure of rules. However, your child may not be ready for a strong team involvement and might do better with swimming, bike-racing, martial arts, or other sports in which the goals are related to self-improvement in time and skills. The competitive nature of football and other team sports may also be too provocative and stressful.

For the verbal child, try the debate team or drama club. Encourage him to run for student office. Let him "fight" for an important political or environmental cause. Channel that strong will into an arena where challenges are appreciated!

Don't Respond Like a
Raging Dragon

It is essential to use the following guidelines when coping with an aggressive child:

●*Be an appropriate example.* Your aggressive child will try your patience and cause you to feel frustrated and angry, but remember, you are the model.

• *Don't retaliate when your child attacks.* If your child provokes you with accusations or swearing, do not take the bait. Develop a sense of humor and deflect the challenges.

• *Be matter-of-fact when you set consequences.*

• *Be lavish in your attention and praise when you see appropriate behavior.*

• *Do not negotiate with a terrorist.* Let your child know the best path to the much-desired power and control is through calm negotiation.

• *Set the stage for negotiations and problem solving.*

• *Begin to "bargain" only when your child is calm and willing to respect limits and boundaries.* Stop all negotiation at once if anger flares or your child begins to blame. Say that as soon as your child is in better control, he can become part of these negotiations himself.

• *Make clear that the goal of negotiation is win-win, not win-lose.* Let your child see you negotiating effectively about the discipline techniques you will use. Teach your child to negotiate with peers.

• *Remain constructive.* Let your child know you expect better and you will respond when you see constructive actions.

When Therapy May Help

Yours is a tough job! Family, friends, teachers, church leaders, everyone can help. Work together to enforce limits. Help each other through tough challenges. Be determined to find positive outlets so that your child can take control with dignity and purpose.

Sometimes despite your best efforts, some children continue to rebel. If your child defies every limit, you know the path of destruction must be stopped. Truancy, drugs, alcohol, fighting, swearing, and refusal to follow rules are all signals that professional help is needed. Therapy can diffuse the control battles between you and your child. Your child can learn to be in control in positive ways. Rather than a warden or referee, you can be a resource and support.

PART VI

LIVING IN PEACE

28

Celebrate! You Are Taming the Dragon

Reading this book shows that you have the energy and motivation to change your family's anger patterns. You probably already have seen positive results as you used, adapted, and fine-tuned the strategies suggested in previous chapters. To maintain momentum and create lasting change, you will need to make these ideas part of your everyday life. This chapter offers guidelines to help you keep the Dragon of Anger tamed in your family, long after you have turned the last page of this book.

Making Up Is Hard To Do

Whew! You've survived another family battle. The Dragon of Anger is safely in its lair. You have guided your family away from the conflict and pointed them toward peace. You have set limits so that your rage and your child's rage can cool. Why, then, does the mood seem so uneasy? Why is someone still sulking? Why are you worrying that, any minute now, another flare-up may flash? Why are you afraid someone will seek revenge? Why do even *you* have the urge to retaliate for all the grief your child's rages have caused?

After a painful or hard-fought conflict, everyone needs time to recover. You, your child or other family members may be feeling ashamed, vulnerable, abandoned, alone, misunderstood, or inadequate. Before peace can return, each of you will need some healing time to recover your energy, your optimism, and your sense of humor.

You are in charge, but maybe you feel wrung dry emotionally, with few resources left. Maybe you're stubbornly hanging on to your own need for control and vindication. During this difficult transition, remember that *you* are the catalyst for change. Unless you can mobilize yourself to move on, you may be setting up a new round of conflict.

Ways to Give Peace a Chance

Stubborn pride and the wish for revenge keep many battles raging and resurfacing. When we are wounded by the Dragon of Anger, it is natural to think mainly of ourselves. We want *our* needs and *our* position to be heard, at any cost. We may think our angry children are selfish, wrong and stubborn. We want them to recognize their errors and put aside their grudges. But your child cannot make peace until *you* do.

Think about the climate in your home after an angry outburst. Are you on the defensive? Do you overreact during the aftermath, as if each new comment is an insult or a renewed attack? If you are feeling inadequate and vulnerable, you may find yourself acting irritable and edgy. You may come on too strong with warnings, criticisms, and lectures. You may simply be making your child feel more ashamed, angry and eager for revenge. Your own "emotional baggage" may be causing you to draw out many current conflicts.

Children operate marvelously in the present. They have a wonderful capacity for moving on with hope and energy. You can take advantage of your child's ability to look forward. You can be instrumental in giving peace a chance.

Soothe the Savage Dragon

If your conflict has been particularly difficult, everyone needs to unwind physically. Give yourselves time alone to read, exercise, clean—time to heal. Your adrenaline has been flowing, and your body needs to get off its overloaded "fight-or-flight" circuit. Be patient. Take the time all of you need. This stage cannot be rushed. Without a sense of calm relief, there can be no healing.

Stop the Blaming

Your internal "tapes" have been switched on. Thoughts race by: *"Those kids are just rude, spoiled little troublemakers!"* *"I'll never get any respect."* *"Just once I wish that kid would obey!"* *"I deserve some time to myself. Why can't these kids ever leave me alone?"*

Your brain can think of a million ways to insult, blame, and mentally retaliate against your out-of-control child. Most of these thoughts unrealistically expect your child to be perfect, or at least reasonable, immediately compliant, and sensitive to your adult needs.

Be realistic. Children, by their nature, are immature, selfish, and demanding. They are not responsible for your peace of mind. They are not responsible for your anger.

Apologize

In any conflict, everyone has a role. Avoid blaming yourself or your child. Take a leadership role. Examine what you could have done differently to avert the conflict. How could you have helped to solve the problem? By being the first to apologize, you do not have to think of yourself as "always being the one to give in." Consider yourself as being the first to offer peace.

Your apology must be sincere. It must be free of criticism and blame, of yourself or your child. Focus on what you wish you would have done and what you would like to do better next time. Your apology becomes a model for your child. Your child learns that everyone makes mistakes. The important thing is to learn from our mistakes.

Then your child should give an apology, which provides an opportunity for learning and self-examination. If he knows that the apology's purpose is to move forward, he will be much more likely to give one. If he worries that the apology will just give the adults more ammunition for lectures or criticism, he will give none. Your child wants to regain a sense of control and hope. A positive, peaceful apology lets that happen.

What if your child does not volunteer an apology? Do not force her. Give her an opportunity. If she does not take advantage of it, let her know when the next opportunity will be. If she does not use her opportunities, extend your cooling-off period. Use fines or restitution periods that can be lifted only after she has made a sincere apology that includes her "peace plan," her ideas to make it better.

Forgive and Forget

Now it is time to forgive yourself. If you sank to the depths of infantile rage, if you did exactly what you promised yourself you would never do, forgive yourself. Nobody's perfect. Your child does not expect you to be perfect. Your child *does* need you to forgive and forget.

You may never truly be able to forget a particularly vicious or wrongful attack. Once you and your child have apologized, however, *put the mistake behind you.* Only another adult can truly understand your pain and be responsible enough to prevent further hurt. Do not expect this from a child. When your child hurts you, it is crucial to let go of the blame and resentment, so that both of you can move forward. Adults need to forget and forgive children's mistakes. We need to be ever hopeful of their ability to do better next time. Restitution gives them a chance to prove themselves worthy again.

Restitution

Atonement. Making amends. Reducing guilt. Shame-busters. Action often helps heal. If you and your child just blew up, do something constructive about it. To take care of your own guilt, prescribe yourself a penance that will help you regain your pride and composure. So much the better if it also involves doing something nice for the person(s) you just hurt with your angry tirade.

Give your child as much control as possible in determining his own plan of restitution. Making amends can be a group or a solo mission. Everyone needs to determine his or her own part. Everyone can make a unique contribution. Draw a happy picture. Clean the mess. Do a favor. Help someone with her work. Create a small gift. Fix someone a favorite snack. How can you help your child make a unique peace offering?

Remember that restitution, like the apology, is a must. It cannot be forced. However, fines and loss of privileges can remain in effect until your child chooses how she will make amends. Younger children need ideas and options. Teens need your confidence that they have the dignity to take control and do it. No child needs smothering, doubts, and criticism at this time. If you remain confident that peace will come, your child can rally.

Make a Peace Plan

Unlike apologies and restitution, which focus on righting the wrongs, your peace plan will focus on *building the "rights."* You can make agreements that not only prevent conflict but also promote peace.

Peace will come only from giving of yourself. Play, hug, laugh. Even the most alienated, angry child has a powerful need to be cared for. The following are suggestions for creating a peace plan for your family:

1. *Understand what each person needs.* If your needs conflict, strike a balance. If you need peace and quiet after a long day, and your teen needs to blast the stereo and talk to his friends, how can you find a compromise? Can you arrange your home so that each of you gets what you need?

If you need a long time alone to mend after an argument, and your child rebounds quickly and wants to talk, how can you both get your needs met? Strike a compromise that becomes part of your peace plan.

2. *Keep it simple. Keep it positive.* Make sure each person has a positive goal to be responsible. Your family can make rules to live by that create a climate of peace.

3. *Consider your danger times.* If you are not a morning person, and anything makes you grumpy before your first cup of coffee, stay away from your child at that time.

4. *Recognize each person's strengths.* Rather than focusing on what not to do, emphasize what each of you *can* do that will work. If we are recognized for what we do well, we can feel proud. If we are given credit for being responsible, we will want to build on our successes. If we focus on what can be done to create a climate of peace, we can rise to the challenge.

5. *Celebrate your successes!* If you and your preschooler make it through the morning rush with your agreed-upon peace, sing his praises. If your rivalrous kids keep their truce, let them revel in a squirt-gun fight. If your rebellious teenager respects your curfew plan, negotiate for more freedom; she has earned it. If you and your children have done what you promised to keep the truce, enjoy! Indulge yourselves in play.

Make Family Time a High Priority

Life is filled with pressures, from the daily grind to the overwhelming pain of death, divorce, or failure. The ache of loss and the exhaustion of stress can disguise themselves as raging Dragons, quick to erupt into uncontrolled torrents of anger and hurt. If, after reading this book and trying many of its strategies, you still are having anger-related problems, you might want to consider what else is going on.

If possible, simplify your life and your commitments. Give yourselves time to relax, unwind, play, hug, read, and renew from the pressures and the stress. You don't have to take an expensive vacation or go out on the town every weekend. Find things at home that you can enjoy. Keep trying. The power of love and humor can overcome the most difficult pressures. Celebrate the power of play.

Set Positive Goals

When you have selected a problem to tackle, think about what you really want to occur. *Be realistic*; you aren't living in a TV sitcom from the 1950s. You and your child are not going to become the perfect family. Focus instead on the positive, and possible, changes you want to replace the destructive anger pattern.

If your child hurls profanity at you each Tuesday morning when you remind him to take out the garbage, what is your positive replacement goal? Can you take a shower during that time and avoid the tirade? Can your child choose another time to empty the garbage cheerfully? If Tuesday morning must be the time, what rewards for calm performance and what fines for cursing are available?

Think through how your child will respond to the different strategies. Be prepared. If you anticipate his response, you can control your own reactions and remain calm and positive, yet firm.

Set small goals for change. You and your child will both feel like exhausted failures if you try to bombard her with numerous expectations for changed behavior. Examine your expectations to be sure they are reasonable.

Your best chance for real change is to help your little (and not so little) child become more gentle and more playful. Remember that, even in fairy tales, the challenge of taming the beast was an epic event. Keep your perspective. Recognize the small steps. Even baby steps build a path to your long-term goal. Savor the victories. Your journey continues; play along the way.

Chart Your Progress

Only you can decide how much time and energy you are willing to commit to the strategies for change offered in this book. As you create a realistic, continuing plan for you and your child, focus first on the suggestions that will help to *prevent* your child's angry outbursts or *reduce* their intensity.

Begin a simple log. Use your date book, daily planner, or calendar. Each day, note your own and your child's displays of anger. Rate their intensity on a one-to-ten scale. Look for any triggers that led to or fueled the outburst. After a week of these observations, study your notes and look for any patterns.

Draw a simple diagram of your family's anger patterns and how they build. Use the Rage Gauge, described in Chapter 18, as a guide. Pinpoint the times and situations that consistently lead to the most frequent and intense problems. Decide which of these is the most important to change. Start simply. Change grows one small step at a time.

Reward Your Family—and Yourself

Celebrate the small accomplishments. If you have stopped anger's chain reaction by taking time to calm yourself, do something nice for yourself. If you have successfully ignored an especially obnoxious bout of whining, make a little sign that sings your own praises. Brag about your progress to a spouse or a friend (not to your child). Better still, brag to your own parents!

When your child first chooses an appropriate way to deal with anger, heap on the recognition and praise. When your teen reaches goals on the contract between you, be proud and let him know it. Create a climate of "expecting good things." Believe that each small step your child takes will help her gather momentum and create more positive behavior. Take time out for play. Create simple ceremonies to mark your accomplishments, however small.

Hang In There!

It's tough being in charge. The responsibility can be exhausting and over-whelming. Conflicts and anger are normal, necessary, and even healthy. You and your child will always get angry. Each of you will face times of stress and strain, in which you will go back to the old patterns of conflict. You may even move into new and negative reactions. This is a *normal* process of growing and changing. Don't be disappointed. *Don't let your child feel discouraged.*

Treat every mistake that you and your child make as learning oppor-tunities. When each of you has calmed down, ask, "What can we do differently next time so that we don't lose control again?" Plan and prac-tice new behaviors, and have several choices, so that each of you will feel unstuck and ready to try a new path.

Recognize and celebrate when your child demonstrates wanting to do what is right. Encourage your child's ability to be free and independ-ent while still being caring and responsible. You cannot Tame the Dragon without mistakes and mishaps, but you *can* concentrate on the progress you will see in yourself and your child.

You are ready to use the skills in this book. You can put your peace plan into place. Your reward will not be a conflict-free future. Your re-ward will come on the day that your children start using ideas from this book on *you!* You can be proud of the example you have provided and of the peacemaker your child can be.

Graduation

When you bought this book, you probably wondered whether your fam-ily could ever change its anger problems. You probably felt overwhelmed and discouraged, but willing to give anything a try. Now look at what you have accomplished!

Before: When your child had a tantrum or screaming fit, you had your own tantrum or screamed right back—or at least felt like doing it.

Now: *You know how to prevent tantrums.* You know that too much pressure and fatigue can trigger a rage. You know that nagging, criticiz-ing, blaming, bombarding, lecturing, or being inconsistent about setting limits can lead to tantrums.

Now: *You know you can stop a tantrum by ignoring it and by setting clear, firm and effective limits.*

Before: When your children ranted and raved to get what they wanted, you often gave in. You were exasperated and afraid that anything you did would just make their behavior worse.

Now: *You know how to teach your children to calm the rage within.* You can guide them in positive ways to express what they want. You can even negotiate with them to set fair rules and consequences. You do not hesitate to set fair limits when needed.

Before: You may have believed that the only way your child could release angry tensions was through punching, screaming, or other tirades.

Now: *You know that children, and adults, need physical release for their tensions and frustrations.* You have structured your family time with plenty of "release times" throughout the week, especially before dinner and during other times when your family's predictable blow-ups occur.

Now: *You have experimented with cool-down techniques that you and your child can use in the heat of angry buildups.* You can signal yourself and your child to try to use them. You know that these strategies won't always work, but they are an important piece of the Dragon puzzle.

Before: You worried that if you set limits on your child's anger outbursts, you would be stifling your child's feelings and possibly damaging his or her self-esteem.

Now: *You know that your child feels ashamed, embarrassed and out of control when the rage builds.* You have new tools to help your child express feelings of all kinds. You know that the heat of an argument is not the time to discuss deep feelings. You are confident that, when you are both calm, you can find new ways to talk things out. You know that your child needs limits and rules about how to express anger to feel safe and loved and to grow up responsibly.

Before: You hated yourself when you did all those things that your parents used to do and that you swore you never would imitate. You felt trapped in the explosive cycle of anger that you and your child seemed to be repeating.

Now: *You can stop the angry cycle.* You see the role you and your child play in the patterns. You can step back, calm yourself, and help your child be calm. Then you can work out the problem.

Before: You could not decide how to discipline your child in the heat of an argument. Everything just seemed to make the conflict worse.

Now: *You have a wide range of discipline techniques for all ages and many types of situations.* You know how to time discipline so that it is effective. You know how to choose discipline so that it becomes one of the ways your child learns to be in control and responsive to others' needs and feelings.

Before: You felt like a referee in the midst of constant battles between your children. You really believed that your kids were driving you crazy.

Now: *You understand that fighting is normal for brothers and sisters.* You know how to structure your family to prevent many conflicts. When the inevitable fight occurs, you can help your children handle it.

Before: Conflicts seemed never-ending. Hurt and revenge always seemed to be lurking. You were focusing your energy on trying to figure out what was fueling the conflicts. You were often afraid of firing up the Dragon, and paralyzed about what to do. Failure seemed inevitable.

Now: *You can enjoy and build on those moments of positive energy.* You know you can manage conflicts. You can negotiate a peace plan. You can joyously celebrate your child's and your own successes.

_____

You truly have graduated. You know that anger is a normal, healthy part of family life. You can face angry feelings and use anger's energy in positive ways to promote family change and understanding. *You are Taming the Dragon!*

Appendix A

SEEKING PROFESSIONAL HELP FOR YOUR CHILD

You may have been worrying for some time, trying everything, and still not believing that you can pull your child out of the quicksand of conflict. Your child's growing rages may have left you frightened at first. Now you may want to harm your child or banish him from the family. Rightfully, you may also be worrying about your own anger.

As you read this book, you may have been thinking, *That sounds good, but we have given up hope that anything will work with our child.* You may feel so confused that you don't know where to start. Asking for professional help is the place to start!

Give your family the commitment to heal. Give yourself credit for having the courage to consult a professional. Take the time to brainstorm with experts who have the knowledge to help you change your family.

Therapy must proceed carefully, with a mental health professional who is well-trained in child development, anger management, family dynamics, parenting skills, and conflict management. Call your local psychological and mental health associations and ask for a referral. Speak to your principal and school counselor about whom they would recommend.

Choosing the Right Therapist

Interview, by phone or in person, the therapists who have been recommended to you. Ask the following questions:

- What training and experience do you have?
- What is your approach to solving anger problems in children?
- What evaluation and assessment procedures will be used to define the problem?
- How will goals for change be set?
- How will parents and teachers be taught to help my child solve his anger problems?
- How will both parents be involved? Be especially clear on this if you are divorced!
- How will my child learn to feel in control of her anger, express her feelings appropriately and solve problems effectively?
- How long will therapy be needed?
- How much will it cost?

The answers to these questions will give you the information you need to choose an effective therapist for your family. You must be comfortable with your therapist's knowledge base, style, and plan. Therapy is hard work; to build trust and an effective working relationship, you need to be working toward the same goals.

Choosing the Right Therapy

An evaluation and consultation will determine if your child needs professional intervention. Individual therapy, however, is seldom effective with a very aggressive child. Family or group therapy provides better structure and strategies to motivate change.

Skill-building is an essential part of the therapy. As a family, you can learn to set specific goals and effective limits. In group therapy, the aggressive child can learn problem-solving and other anger-management skills. Practicing these in the safety of the group will give your child a sense of competence and status. Your child can then teach your family and lead you toward change.

The evaluation or a trial period of therapy can determine whether your aggressive child can be helped to change within his or her home and school settings. Some children need alternative school and living environments, which provide more structure, clear and fair limits, and intensive help for the child to monitor and change his or her behavior. Never use these options as a punishment or threat to your child. Special schools or placements are opportunities for change—for all of you. Select a program with active family involvement. This will give you new skills for coping and help your child come home to you more quickly.

Beginning the Real Work

With the decision to enter therapy and the choice of a therapist made, your work is just beginning. You and your child will set goals for change together. With change, anxiety and conflict can build. Your therapist should help you learn new tools for dealing with conflict. As an adviser, the therapist should help you and your child become the masters of change.

Remember, before you can talk safely about feelings your family may need to resolve, the explosions need to stop. Once you have mastered the skills to stay calm, then therapy can address issues such as loss, hurt, rejection, disappointment, and frustration. Beware of therapy that moves into these potentially threatening issues too quickly. Build a climate of safety first.

When children have anger problems, their rage is often triggered at school as well. Do not feel embarrassed to bring teachers and other school staff in as part of the team. Change can come more quickly with everyone working together. Do be clear with your child and your therapist about what information needs to stay confidential within the family and what can be shared with the school. Do recognize that the teacher's strengths and anger-management style may well be different from your own. Create a plan that can build upon everyone's strengths and can give your child the tools to succeed in controlling his anger.

Many times children with excessive anger outbursts at school have personal problems that need to be addressed within the family therapy. Often, however, the anger problems are fueled by peer or classroom difficulties. Your therapist may help devise a plan to correct these difficulties.

Appendix B
PARENTS, SCHOOLS, AND COMMUNITIES TOGETHER

The environment we provide our children has a powerful effect on whether they will be raging tyrants or peacemakers. Our communities create children who can deal with anger constructively or destructively. The examples we provide will determine how our children will manage conflict. The climate of our communities will shape the future of our children and our world.

After reading this book, you undoubtedly are more in control of providing a home that fosters healthy solutions to anger problems. But what about all the violence our children see every day? How can we continue to provide positive examples of conflict resolution when our kids are exposed to so much cruelty, hurt, and destruction in this world? Is what we do in our little corner of the world really going to make a difference? You bet!

Children learn from direct experience. The emotional climate in their home, school, and neighborhood will indeed make a difference. Children have remarkable inner resources and the capacity for moral strength. If given the proper love, support, and training, they will learn to let their innate goodness guide them.

Robert Coles, a renowned psychiatrist and author of *The Moral Life of Children* (Boston: The Atlantic Monthly Press, 1986), has witnessed children's resilient power to overcome the violence, racism, and conflict of a society that can be vicious and unfair.

Dr. Coles chronicles his work with a black girl named Ruby in New Orleans in the early 1960s: Angry crowds hurled cruel and abusive slurs at first-grader Ruby each day as federal agents escorted her to her newly desegregated classroom. Her bravery and her belief that good would prevail came not only from family support but also from a powerful inner courage. As enraged crowds seemed ready to consume her with their anger, young Ruby responded by praying for them. Her spirit of forgiveness, her determination that might does not make right, and the support of the civil rights movement made success possible.

Thirty years later, our society is still beset by prejudice and its aftermath: riots, delinquency, and gang violence. Race and class tensions erupt into destructive acts of rage. Child abuse is on the rise. More and more teens are angry at the world as they leave school, ill-prepared for their own future. TV and movies, those powerful socializers of children, spew out daily doses of destruction and violence. TV comedies seem to undermine parents' role as powerful, helpful resolvers of problems and conflicts. Schools sometimes seem like battlegrounds, not playgrounds or havens of academic and moral learning.

How can we be effective in changing the climate of violence? How can our children have hope that they can resolve conflicts in their world? Does peace really have a chance?

We—parents, schools, and communities together—need to become leaders for peace. We can take control of the environment our children live in every day. We can create a climate of peace by turning off the TV (or at least changing the channel.) We can vow to stop the cycle of violence within our own homes. Neighbors can band together to keep each other safe. Communities can develop mediation programs to settle conflicts without aggression.

Schools can include conflict-resolution and violence-prevention programs. Principals can make sure that staff are trained as mediators to guide children in solving their conflicts productively. Churches, organizations, and civic groups can develop mentor programs so that children without strong examples of hope, commitment, and safety can have adults dedicated to their future and willing to guide them toward responsible choices.

What You Can Do at Home

Create a climate where your family manages anger fairly and balances the needs and rights of each member. By using the strategies in this book, you will find it easier to change your little corner of the world. But what about the unknown Dragons of Anger your child is exposed to away from you? What influence and control do you really have? What can you do to help when your child becomes tangled in vicious conflicts at school and with friends? Will your role be adversarial, fueling revenge and polarizing through blaming and taking sides? Will your role as a parent be as an advocate, to promote your child's ability to solve problems confidently and peacefully? Advocate or adversary: That is your choice.

If you have become alienated from relatives, if feuds and conflicts boil over regularly, you might also explore mediation. *Family mediators* are trained to focus on specific problems and to find solutions. Compromise can save face and let everyone win a little. Healing and peace can happen. Unlike intensive therapy approaches, family mediators do not uncover raw feelings and do not reopen old wounds. Long hours of therapy may not be necessary; short-term solutions, focused on mediation, can be effective.

Mediators can help parents and angry teens settle disputes about curfews, car privileges, who pays for what, and other conflicts. Mediators can help parents settle disputes about possessions, responsibilities, and ownership of family treasures. Mediators can help divorced couples negotiate the treacherous waters of visitation schedules or handling a wedding or bar mitzvah.

Give peace a chance. If you are at war with family, friends, or neighbors, try a different way. Your community social services often offer low-cost mediation. Bar associations can refer you to mediators who need to consider legal issues. Mental health associations can refer you to mediators who have training in dispute-resolution of emotional and family issues.

If you can mend your ways, you will become a powerful example to your child that people can master the Dragon of Anger. Peace, or at least a cease-fire, can rule.

What Schools Can Do

Too often, our solution to kids' conflicts is to create a military-type atmosphere at school, by increased monitoring of the students and more rules, regulations, and discipline. Sometimes, when anarchy has reigned, this is necessary. But children need to have some control, too. They can learn to solve many of their own problems, if given the tools and the opportunity. Peer-mediation programs give kids positive strategies to resolve disputes and monitor themselves in the classroom and on the playground. Violence-prevention courses teach kids the skills to solve problems and settle conflicts without aggression.

Peer-Mediation Programs

Throughout the country, teachers, counselors, and parents have teamed to establish programs that allow children to solve many of their own conflicts. Peer mediators are trained in problem-solving strategies. Sometimes children are chosen to become peer mediators because they are leaders; more often they are chosen because these are the skills the child lacks. Learning problem-solving skills will give kids the tools to handle their problems and will offer them newfound status with the group.

Peer mediators are trained to watch for signs of brewing trouble. Their role is to encourage kids in conflict to find other things to do. If conflict still builds, they call a truce. Each side must listen to the other completely, without comment. Each side must state what it needs and what it can do to solve the problem. Both sides develop a compromise plan of action and agree to follow the plan. The goal is for each child to win.

School districts have been active in developing and implementing peer-mediation programs. Contact your school counselor or principal to see what is available in your community. Following are examples of the types of programs that are available nationally.

The *New York City Schools and Educators for Social Responsibility* have worked to establish conflict-resolution programs. They have combined peer-mediation training with educational materials and videos to give teachers and students the skills to prevent conflicts and to mediate solutions. The *Resolving Conflict Creatively Program* information can be obtained by writing: 163 Third Avenue, #239, New York, NY 10003.

Educators for Social Responsibility is an organization you may want to join. It provides resources and educational materials for promoting peacemaking in our schools and ultimately in our communities and our world. Write to the organization at 23 Garden Street, Cambridge, MA 02138. Or call 1-800-370-2515 for a catalog and membership information.

The Seattle, Washington, schools have developed a program called *Second Step*. For grades K through 8, curriculum and video combinations are available by writing the Committee for Children, 172 20th Avenue, Seattle, WA 98122. Consultants are available to train your school staff; call 800-634-4449.

In San Francisco, the *Community Board Program* has developed conflict-resolution resources for schools and youth. *Conflict Resolution* curricula for grades K through 12 are available. Conflict-manager training materials help schools begin peer-mediation programs. Consultants from their programs provide workshops to train teachers in how to establish conflict-management programs. Write to the Community Board Program, 1540 Market Street, Suite 490, San Francisco, CA 94102.

Violence-Prevention Curricula

School staff and parents can work together to make anger control, mediation, and positive problem-solving priorities. Many school districts have begun programs that encourage children to handle their disputes in positive ways. These programs range from simple rules to live by to the purchase of extensive curricula that are taught in each grade.

Extensive curricula have been developed to teach children of all ages to solve problems without violence. Debra Prothrow-Stith, a physician and public health educator, has documented that violence is the number one public health problem in this country today. Teens are killing each other in record numbers. Gang activity and other senseless violence continues to rise. Many children are being reared in poverty, abuse, and discrimination. Many are full of rage and know no productive ways to solve their problems.

No wonder so many children feel hopeless and angry. Many adults do, as well. These children's problems are our societal problems. But we can do something. In Deborah Prothrow-Stith's book, *Deadly Consequences: How Violence Is Destroying Our Teenage Population and a Plan to Begin Solving the Problem* (New York: HarperCollins, 1991), readers can find proposed solutions and an extensive array of curricula resources that can give children, and even very violent teens, the tools they need to resolve conflicts without aggression. The cycle of violence can be stopped.

Dr. Prothrow-Stith's *Violence Prevention Curriculum for Adolescents* is available by writing the Education Development Center, Inc., 55 Chapel Street, Newton, MA 02160.

The PREPARE Curriculum: Teaching Prosocial Competencies, by Arnold Goldstein, provides an extensive review of training resources and strategies that can be used by teachers. Broad in its focus, this book covers problem solving, anger control, moral reasoning, stress management, empathy, and interpersonal skills. Write to Research Press, 2612 North Mattis Avenue, Champaign, IL 61821.

Research Press also publishes a video training program for parents and teens, which can help them learn to manage anger. Developed by the Institute for Mental Health Initiatives, the *RETHINK Method* gives tools for developing self-control and "talk it out—work it out" strategies.

Another video resource is *You Can Choose*, produced by Elkind and Sweet Communication, Inc. The ten-video series teaches personal responsibility, the ability to get along with others, and conflict-management skills. Problem-solving situations are presented as a springboard for class discussion. Write to the William Gladden Foundation, 7 Bridge Street, Cameron, WV 26033 for a resource catalog.

BeCool is an anger-management and violence-prevention video curriculum. Teens learn to cope with teasing, criticism, and bullying, and to manage their anger by staying cool. It is available through the James Stanfield Publishing Company, Drawer B, P.O. Box 41058, Santa Barbara, CA 93140.

Another video resource for adolescents is the group training program developed by Jim Larson, Ph.D. *Think First: Anger and Aggression Management Training for Secondary Level Students* teaches teens to gain positive power through problem solving and anger control. Write to Dr.

Jim Larson, Psychology Department, University of Wisconsin, Whitewater, WI 93190.

What the Community Can Do

Studies of violence show that, however "senseless" the outcome seems, there often has been a history of conflict and a buildup of the tension that finally exploded. Teens often overreact to minor slights and perceive hostile intent, even if there is none. Very violent teens continually think the world is out to get them. They respond accordingly by lashing out at the unfairness around them. Many gain a sense of status and importance by being tough.

Most teen conflicts are played out to an audience of other teens, who not only observe the buildup of tension but also help to increase it. Rumors fly. Friends take sides. Loyalties shift. The drama builds. Boys may feel locked into the obligation to defend their honor or the honor of their girlfriend. Girls may feel they must defend their status within the group or use whatever means necessary to keep their boyfriend. These are age-old struggles, yet in Greek tragedy, the chorus actually provides a description of the events. Today's modern teen audience echoes and amplifies the conflict; violence can escalate quickly.

Violence can erupt when there seems to be no other solution. Sadly, many teens have never learned other ways to handle problems. Even within our most violent communities, kids do want options. Communities do want alternatives to aggression and destruction. People do want a way out. There is hope if the tools are available.

Mentor Programs

Grass-roots efforts in communities across the country are offering helping hands to kids in need—not a handout, but truly a human hand. Adults are working one on one with kids who need an ally, an advocate, a surrogate parent, a conscience, a voice, or a guide. These mentors provide caring and hope. They provide an example of what the future can be: a productive life in which hard work, responsibility, and personal connections can lead to dignity and, in many programs, a job. When lonely or disadvantaged kids have someone to believe in them, they can begin to believe in themselves.

The *Big Brother/Big Sister* program has provided countless adult friends to children in need of support. An advocate can make a difference. Exposure to people who care and who can use nonviolent means to settle conflicts can open a child's eyes. For kids who have dropped out of school and are struggling to stay out of the cycle of illegal, immoral, and violent survival tactics, an advocate can literally save a life.

The *"I Have a Dream"* program has provided mentors and guaranteed college scholarship money to kids who can keep the commitment to graduate. Making a personal commitment can give kids a positive direction and a crucial sense of self-esteem, which helps them keep their self-respect and reduces the risk of rage erupting into violence. For the mentor, making a commitment to a child can offer deep personal rewards and can give us all hope that our violent society can change.

Community Mediation

How do you and your neighbors solve problems? Do neighborhood feuds simmer for years? Could skirmishes erupt into open warfare with only slight provocation? Are lawsuits brewing? Or is there open discussion of issues? Do you respect each other's rights? Do you take personal responsibility for your actions and share responsibility for the group?

The climate in our communities does affect our children. They watch us and learn. They can learn to be warriors or peacemakers. Sometimes we need to learn the tools as much as our children do. Mediation programs can help adults resolve disputes productively, from dealing with barking dogs and broken fences to mending the wounds of racist attacks. If your community seems more like a war zone than a peaceful family center, explore these mediation services.

If you would like more information about community mediation resources, contact the *Conflict Resolution Center International*, 7101 Hamilton Avenue, Pittsburgh, PA 15208-1828. CRCI provides resources, conflict-resolution experts, and knowledge worldwide to resolve disputes peacefully. Whether your problems are neighborhood, school, racial, religious, ethnic, or business related, this group has a referral base of mediation experts and a resource library to tackle a wide range of problems.

We Can All Be Peacemakers

The Oregon Peace Institute offers workshops, mediation referrals, books, games, curriculum materials, and videos for sale or loan to the public. For resources, or information about establishing an institute, write The Oregon Peace Institute, The Galleria, Suite 520, 921 SW Morrison, Portland, OR 97205. Your community can unite to teach, promote, and live the path to peace.

We can all be peacemakers. Teachers and parents can bring the skills of peacemaking to life for children: accepting self and others, communicating effectively, resolving conflicts, and understanding intercultural differences. Give peace a chance.

Recommended Reading

Personal Change

Averill, James. "Studies on Anger and Aggression." *American Psychologist* 39(1983):1145–60. An excellent article summarizing the theoretical and research studies historically related to emotion.

Bernstein, Albert, Ph.D., and Sydney Rozen. *Dinosaur Brains*. New York: Wiley. 1989. A self-help book for adults that addresses interpersonal problems that can occur in the workplace. Covers anger as well as other emotional responses.

Brodsky, Gary. *The Art of Getting Even: The Do-It-Yourself Justice Manual*. Secaucus, NJ: Castle Books, 1990. Use humor and imagination to relieve your frustrations and come out a winner.

Ellis, Albert. *Anger: How to Live With and Without It*. Secaucus, NJ: Citadel Press, 1977. The premiere work for adults on how to use cognitive control strategies (or rational emotive strategies, as the author calls them) to manage anger.

Lerner, Harriet Goldhor. *The Dance of Anger: A Woman's Guide to Changing the Patterns of Intimate Relationships*. New York: Harper and Row Publishers, 1985. An excellent volume to provide insight into the dynamic processes that influence our expression of emotion in intimate, family relationships.

McKay, Matthew, Peter Rogers, and Judith McKay. *When Anger Hurts: Quieting the Storm Within*. Oakland, CA: New Harbinger Publications, 1989. Understand your anger and build the skills to change from destructive patterns to healthy resolution.

Novaco, Raymond. *Anger Control: Cognitive Behavioral Interven-*

tions and Cognitive Behavioral Therapy. Edited by T. J. Forey and D. Rath-jen. New York: Plenum Press, 1978. Novaco is a pioneer in research and clinical intervention for adults. His work helps readers identify triggers of anger and the thinking errors that intensify anger reactions and offers ways to use cognitive control to express anger more appropriately.

Strayhorn, J. M. *Talking It Out: A Guide to Effective Communication and Problem Solving*. Champaign, IL: Research Press Co., 1977. Clear and simple strategies for couples to master expressing feelings, negotiation, and problem solving.

Tavris, Carol. *Anger: The Misunderstood Emotion*. New York: Simon and Schuster, 1983. A readable review of the cultural context of anger. Offers insight into various therapy interventions available to help adults change.

Warren, Neil. *Make Anger Your Ally: Harnessing One of Your Most Powerful Emotions*. Brentwood, TN: Wolgemuth & Hyatt Pub., 1990. Self-help at its most practical and realistic.

Weisinger, Hendric. *Dr. Weisinger's Anger Workbook*. New York: Morrow, 1985. A self-help book intended for adults, which could also be used by older, motivated adolescents. Assists readers to examine their own anger styles and triggers. Offers many exercises to practice alternative ways of thinking and reacting to anger-triggering situations.

Child Development and Special Challenges

Chess, Stella, and Alexander Thomas. *Temperament in Clinical Practice*. New York: Guilford Press, 1986. A textbook intended for professional use but an excellent review of the issues.

Ingersoll, Barbara. *Your Hyperactive Child: A Parent's Guide to Coping with Attention Deficit Disorder*. New York: Doubleday, 1988. How parents and teachers can chart a path for effective diagnosis and treatment of hyperactive children. Practical and professional advice to steer you clear of charlatans.

Kurcinka, Mary. *Your Spirited Child*. New York: Harper Perennial, 1991. A guide for parents whose children are more intense, sensitive, perceptive, persistent, and energetic. Strategies for channeling a difficult, strong-willed child in a positive direction. How to prevent and cope with anger-provoking situations.

Parens, Henri. *Aggression in Our Children: Coping With It Constructively*. Northvale, NJ: Jason Aronson, Publisher, 1987. Child development of aggressive tendencies and what a parent can do to understand.

Tobin, L. *What Do You Do with a Child Like This? Inside the Lives of Troubled Children*. Duluth, MN: Pfeifer-Hamilton Publishers, 1991. A notebook of thoughts, anecdotes, and techniques for teachers and parents who work with especially troubled children.

Turecki, S., and L. Tonner. *The Difficult Child*. New York: Bantam Books, 1985. A help for parents who struggle with difficult, irritable children. Understand more about temperament, learn to prevent conflicts, and manage explosions.

Moral Development

Damon, William. *The Moral Child: Nurturing Children's Natural Moral Growth*. New York: Free Press, 1988.

Kohlberg, Lawrence. *Essays on Moral Development, Vol. 2, The Psychology of Moral Development*. New York: Harper & Row, 1984.

Schulman, Michael, and Eva Mekler. *Bringing Up a Moral Child: A New Approach for Teaching Your Child to be Kind, Just and Responsible*. Reading, MA: Addison-Wesley, 1985.

Selman, R. L. *The Growth of Interpersonal Understanding*. New York: Academic Press, 1980.

Books to Read to Young Children

Berenstain, Stan and Jan. *The Berenstain Bears Get in a Fight*. New York: Random House, 1982. The oh-so-familiar bears solve conflicts simply and positively.

Crary, Elizabeth. *Dealings with Feelings* series: *I'm Frustrated; I'm Mad*. Seattle: Parenting Press, 1992. Fun, gamelike books to teach preschool and early elementary children to solve problems and handle feelings.

Erickson, Karen, and Maureen Roffey. *I Was So Mad*. New York: Viking Kestrel, 1987. Children learn that it is OK to be mad, as long as they are in control and do not hurt others.

Leonard, Marcia. *How I Feel Angry*. New York: Bantam Books, 1988. Describes, in simple terms, situations that make people angry and how to cope with angry feelings.

Lindgren, Astrid. *Lotta on Troublesome Street*. New York: Macmillan & Co. A grumpy morning escalates from control battles with Mom to a child running away from home. The child chooses to come home and learns he can be in control of his food and his clothes in more positive ways.

Preston, Edna. *The Temper Tantrum Book*. New York: Viking Press, 1969. Animal characters throw tantrums because of things they did or could not do.

Sendak, Maurice. *Where the Wild Things Are*. New York: Harper and

Row, 1963. The classic tale of an angry boy who dreams that he has gone to a land of monsters who love him and make him their king. He is happy with his power, until he gets homesick.

Sharmat, Marjorie. *Attila the Angry.* New York: Holiday House, 1985. With the help of Angry Animals Anonymous, Attila the squirrel learns how to control his angry behavior.

Simon, Norma. *I Was So Mad!* Niles, IL: Albert Whitman & Co., 1979. This story identifies triggers of anger, such as frustration, anxiety, humiliation and loss of control. Boys and girls learn that anger is normal and learn a song to use to cope.

Watson, Jane, and Robert Switzer. *Sometimes I Get Angry.* Topeka, KS: Meninger Press, 1986. A simple, expressive story that helps children understand that anger is normal. The book also provides guidance to parents: Often preschoolers become angry and frustrated because they cannot yet, or adults do not let them, master new skills.

Zolotow, Charlotte. *The Hating Book.* New York: Harper & Row, 1989. Two girls learn to put aside their stubbornness, think of the other's perspective and take positive steps to remain friends.

Books for School-Age Children

Carlson, Nancy. *Loudmouth George and the Sixth-Grade Bully.* Carolrhoda Books, 1983. George and his friend find a creative way to deal with the bully who steals his lunch.

Hanrahan, Brendan. *My Sisters Love My Clothes.* Chappaqua, NY: Perry Heights Press, 1992. Kids learn to solve a never-ending source of conflict—possessions.

Kaufman, Gershen, and Lev Raphael. *Stick Up for Yourself: Every Kid's Guide to Personal Power and Self-Esteem.* Minneapolis, MN: Free Spirit Publishers, 1990. Preteens and teens learn that you can be strong and in control without aggression. Assertiveness skills made easy. Confidence builds self-esteem.

Schmidt, Fran, and Alice Friedman. *Fighting Fair for Families.* Miami, FL: Peace Press, 1989. Kids and parents learn ways to emotionally disengage from conflict and to solve problems cooperatively. A poster of Rules for Fighting Fair can help you and your child remember to put anger control skills into practice. Write to Peace Education Foundation, Inc., P.O. 191153, Miami Beach, FL 33119.

Webster-Doyle, Terrance. *Tug of War: Peace Through Understanding Conflict. Facing the Double-Edged Sword: The Art of Karate for Young People. Why is Everybody Always Picking on Me? A Guide to Handling Bullies. Fighting the Invisible Enemy: Understanding the Effects of Conditioning.* Middlebury, VT: Atrium Publications, 1992. Four books for school-age children to learn the tools for peacemaking.

Books for Teens

Berg, Berthold. *The Anger Control Workbook: Exercises to Develop Anger Control Skills.* Cognitive Counseling Resources, 1990. A training, exercise book for teens.

Cole, Jim. *Thwarting Anger: A View of How We Keep Anger Alive.* Mill Valley, CA: Ed and Janet Reynolds, Publishers, 1992. An illustrated guide to anger triggers and the thinking errors that compound angry feelings. Identifies destructive patterns and presents them in the light of the hurt they create. Offers positive coping strategies.

Hopper, N. J. *Ape Ears and Beaky.* New York: Avon Books. Thirteen-year-old Scott struggles to learn to control his temper, but not before it has led to trouble, including dismissal from one baseball team, humiliation on another, and involvement with his enemy, Beaky, in a plan to catch some professional thieves.

Levy, Barrie. *In Love and In Danger: A Teen's Guide to Breaking Free of Abusive Relationships.* Seattle, WA: Seal Press, 1993. Gives teens strategies for handling anger and preventing violence in dating relationships.

Packer, Alex. *Bringing Up Parents: The Teenager's Handbook.* Minneapolis, MN: Free Spirit Publishing, 1992. Teens can take control to gain the privileges and freedom they want—without fighting.

Vedral, J. L. *My Parents Are Driving Me Crazy.* New York: Ballantine Books, 1986. How teens can cope with their anger and frustration at having a parent.

Parents' Anger

Faber, Adele, and Elaine Mazlish. *Liberated Parents, Liberated Children: Your Guide to a Happier Family.* New York: Avon Books, 1990. Parents discuss their own struggles to control their anger to become calm and confident.

Samalin, Nancy. *Love and Anger, the Parental Dilemma.* New York: Viking, 1991. Parents learn to cope with their own guilt, debunk myths that disappoint, and lovingly break anger patterns.

Parent-Child Communication

Faber, Adele, and Elaine Mazlish. *How to Talk So Kids Will Listen and Listen So Kids Will Talk.* New York: Rawson-Wade, 1980, and Avon Books. An immensely popular book because it speaks from the heart and offers practical tips.

Forgatch, Marion, and Gerald Patterson. *Parents and Adolescents Living Together: Family Problem Solving.* Eugene, OR: Castalia Publishing,

1989. Negotiate a cooperative environment with your teen through communication and problem-solving skills.

Shure, M. B., and G. Spivak. *Problem Solving Techniques in Child Rearing.* San Francisco: Jossey-Bass, 1978. The pioneers of problem solving direct professionals to a successful approach for families.

Effective Discipline

Bodenhamer, Gary. *Back in Control: How to Get Your Children to Behave.* New York: Prentice Hall, 1983. Regaining authority and setting fair limits on older children and teens.

Gathercoal, Forrest. *Judicious Parenting.* San Francisco: Caddo Gap Press, 1992. Beyond rewards and punishment, establish a democratic family life.

Patterson, Gerald. *Families.* Champaign, IL: Research Press, 1974. A great yet simple volume to help parents organize and use discipline and positive behavior-change programs.

Samalin, Nancy. *Loving Your Child Is Not Enough: Positive Discipline that Works.* New York: Penguin, 1988. Discipline is teaching. Parents can be loving and firm.

Whitham, Cynthia. *Win the Whining War and Other Skirmishes: A Family Peace Plan.* Los Angeles: Perspective Publishers, 1991. Practical solutions for those situations that drive every parent crazy.

Cooperation and Conflict Resolution for Families

Ames, L. B., and C. C. Haber. *He Hit Me First.* New York: Warner Books, 1982. An excellent, practical book to help parents understand why siblings fight. Prevention and intervention strategies are simple and effective.

Crary, Elizabeth. *Kids Can Cooperate: A Practical Guide to Teaching Problem Solving.* Seattle: Parenting Press, 1984. Presents typical triggers of children's conflict. Dialogue offers ideas for how a child can respond. Extensive exercises teach preschool children negotiation and problem-solving skills.

Fisher, Roger, and Scott Brown. *Getting Together: Building Relationships as We Negotiate.* New York: Viking Penguin, 1988. A guide to negotiating, nurturing, and sustaining enduring relationships—in business, between friends, and in the family.

McGinnis, Kathleen, and James McGinnis. *Parenting for Peace and Justice: Ten Years Later.* Maryknoll, NY: Orbis Books. From a personal level, to the family, to the world, you can find relevant and meaningful ways to promote peace.

McGinnis, Kathleen, and Barbara Oelhlberg. *Starting out Right: Nurturing Young Children as Peacemakers*. New York: Crossroad Publishing, 1991. Clarify your family's values about violence, racism, sexism, ageism, and nationalism that undermine the struggle for peace and justice. Find peace in your family and promote justice in your world.

Wilt, Joy. *Handling Your Disagreements*. Columbus, OH: Weekly Reader Books. Children can use these ideas to help them with conflict resolution.

Games

Berg, Berthold. *The Anger Game*. Cognitive Counseling Resources, 3430 S. Dixie Dr., Dayton, OH 45439. A board game for children ages 7 to 14, which teaches assertiveness and problem-solving skills to deal with conflicts.

Give Peace a Chance. Fresno, CA: Peace Works, Inc., 1987. A game of international relations and conflict resolution.

Luvmour, Sambhava, and Josette. *Everyone Wins! Cooperative Games and Activities*. Philadelphia: Center for Educational Guidance and New Society Publishers. Games for all ages and all sizes of children's groups, which promote sharing and cooperation rather than competition and conflict.

Masheder, Mildred. *Let's Play Together*. London: Green Print, 1989. Over three hundred games and sports that put cooperation before competition—and make everyone a winner! A wide diversity of interests, ages, and numbers of players are sure to learn from and enjoy these games.

Thompson, Lynn. *Angry Animals*. Rainbow Kids, P.O. Box 4562, St. Paul, MN 55104. A board game for children ages 5 to 12 to teach healthy choices for handling anger-provoking situations.

Programs and Curricula for Conflict Resolution and Problem Solving

Cheatham, A. *Directory of School Mediation And Conflict Resolution Programs*. Amherst, MA: National Association of Mediation in Education, 1988.

Drew, Naomi. *Learning the Skills of Peacemaking: An Activity Guide for Elementary-Age Children on Communicating, Cooperating and Resolving Conflict*. Rolling Hills Estates, CA: Jalmar Press, 1987. Excellent activities and guidelines for classroom intervention. Let peace begin with one and expand to the community and the world.

Feindler, E. L., and R. B. Ecton. *Adolescent Anger Control: Cognitive Behavioral Techniques*. New York: Pergammon Press, 1986. The best summary of cognitive behavioral interventions. For the professional group leader, provides detailed protocols for group training in anger control.

Goldstein, Arnold. *The PREPARE Curriculum*. Champaign, IL: Research Press, 1989. The best thorough review of classroom intervention strategies for teachers, counselors, and special educators. Excellent, practical classroom exercises to teach anger management, problem solving, and social skills. Straightforward literature reviews.

Higgins, Pat. *Helping Kids Handle Anger: Teaching Self-Control*. The ASSIST Program, Sopris West, Inc. 1140 Boston Ave., Longmont, CA 80501. A curriculum for primary and secondary students that teaches it's OK to be mad; it's not OK to be mean.

Jackson, N. F., D. A. Jackson, and C. Monroe. *Getting Along with Others: Teaching Social Effectiveness to Children: Skill Lessons and Activities*. Champaign, IL: Research Press, 1983. A valuable resource for educators to teach children appropriate communication and negotiation skills. The ideas are simple and intended to be used for group instruction. Parents may wish to gather constructive ideas for inclusion in a special-needs child's individualized education.

Judson, Stephanie. *A Manual on Nonviolence and Children*. Philadelphia: New Society Publishers, 1977. Create an atmosphere in which children and adults can resolve their problems and conflicts nonviolently. Session plans, role-plays, exercises, and games to teach the skills of peacemaking.

Oregon Peace Institute. *Elementary Curriculum Guide*. Oregon Peace Institute, 921 SW Morrison, Portland, OR 97205. A resource guide to help parents and teachers discover materials to use in educating children in conflict resolution and nuclear age issues.

Schmidt, Fran, and Alice Friedman. *Creative Conflict Solving for Kids*. Miami Beach, FL: Peace Works, 1985. This curriculum challenges students (grades 5–9) to deal creatively and constructively with conflict. Worksheets and experiential learning tasks are provided, which can be integrated into social studies, science, and language curriculum.

Schmidt, Fran, Alice Friedman, Brunt Elyse, and Theresa Solotoff. *Peace-making Skills for Little Kids*. Miami Beach, FL: Peace Works, 1993. Preschool teachers can establish a nurturing environment that promotes conflict resolution. Classroom layout, daily activities, and reading materials are integrated into a skill building program.

Schmidt, Fran, Alice Friedman, and Jean Marvel. *Mediation for Kids: Kids in Dispute Resolution*. Miami Beach, FL: Peace Works, 1990. Teach students to be peer mediators. Using mediation skills kids help other kids talk out problems and come to a win/win solution.

Shure, Myrna. *I Can Problem Solve (ICPS): An Interpersonal Cognitive Problem-Solving Program for Children*. Champaign, IL: Research Press,

1992. Three editions for three age groups. Lessons incorporate games, stories, puppets, and role-plays to teach problem-solving skills and how teachers can integrate these concepts into reading, math, science and social studies curricula.

Wichert, Suzanne. *Keeping the Peace: Practicing Cooperation and Conflict Resolution with Preschoolers.* Philadelphia: New Society Publishers, 1989. Parents, child care providers, and teachers can establish a learning environment in which preschoolers learn to resolve conflict peacefully among themselves.

Also see Appendix B: Parents, Schools, and Communities Together for other resources.

Index

About the Authors

Meg Eastman, Ph.D., is a clinical psychologist in Portland, Oregon, who specializes in interventions with high-conflict families experiencing divorce, abuse, and difficult-to-manage children.

She is a coowner of the Children's Program, an interdisciplinary clinic with a regional reputation for providing consultation, training, assessment, and therapy for families and professionals dealing with difficult children.

Her book is based on material drawn from her own teachings and clinical practice, as well as ideas from her colleagues in education, psychology, communication, and medicine.

Dr. Eastman is frequently consulted by parents, school authorities, caseworkers, and mental health professionals for help in dealing with children whose behavior seems beyond control. She is a frequent speaker and workshop leader for schools, parent groups, law enforcement personnel, and mental health professionals.

Her practical suggestions and realistic solutions have strengthened her professional reputation for combining sensitivity with common sense. A parent who had been struggling with an emotionally explosive daughter for years recently told Dr. Eastman, "We thought we had tried everything. You are the first one who has given us practical information and tools to help our child change herself."

Another family, after consulting her, said, "We are no longer afraid of anger. We can express it without fear [that] we're starting World War III."

Sydney Craft Rozen is a writer and editor based in Bothell, Washington. She is coauthor, with Albert J. Bernstein, Ph.D, of *Dinosaur Brains: Dealing with All Those Impossible People at Work* and *Neanderthals at Work: How People and Politics Can Drive You Crazy . . . and What You Can Do About Them* (New York: John Wiley & Sons, Inc., 1992).

She also was editor for and contributed to the best-selling *Sidetracked Home Executives* by Pam Young and Peggy Jones (Warner Books), and to the self-help book, *The Happiness File*, by the same authors. She has been a newspaper writer and features editor and is a former college instructor of English and journalism.